INTO THE
WHITE

INTO THE
WHITE

INTO THE WHITE

SCOTT'S ANTARCTIC ODYSSEY

JOANNA GROCHOWICZ

ALLEN&UNWIN
SYDNEY·MELBOURNE·AUCKLAND·LONDON

First published by Allen & Unwin in 2017

Allen & Unwin
83 Alexander Street
Crows Nest NSW 2065
Australia
Phone: (61 2) 8425 0100
Email: info@allenandunwin.com
Web: www.allenandunwin.com

A Cataloguing-in-Publication entry is available from the National Library of Australia
www.trove.nla.gov.au

ISBN 978 1 76029 365 9

Teachers' notes available from www.allenandunwin.com

Cover and text design by Joanna Hunt
Cover and text illustrations by Sarah Lippett
Set in ITC Legacy Serif pt 11/17.5 by Midland Typesetters

Printed in Australia in December 2017 at the SOS Print + Media Group,
10 9 8 7 6 5 4

www.facebook.com/intothewhitenovel

For Honey

ROBERT
FALCON SCOTT

LAWRENCE
'TITUS' OATES

EDWARD
'UNCLE BILL' WILSON

CECIL
MEARES

APSLEY
CHERRY - GARRARD

HENRY
'BIRDIE' BOWERS

EDWARD
EVANS

EDGAR
'TAFF' EVANS

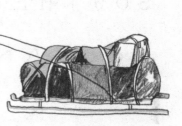

THOMAS
CLISSOLD

HERBERT
PONTING

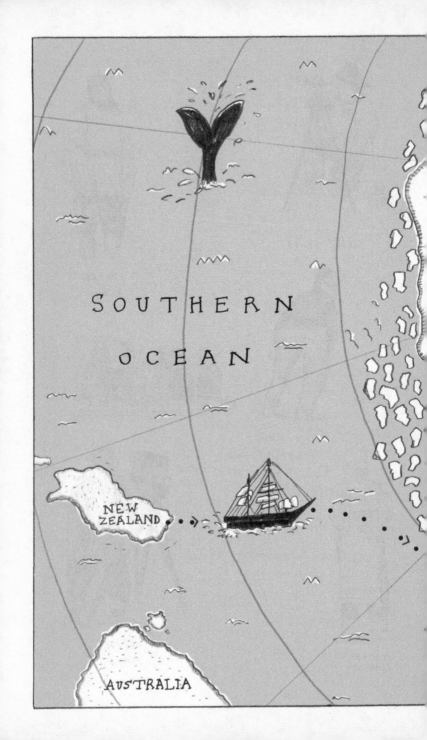

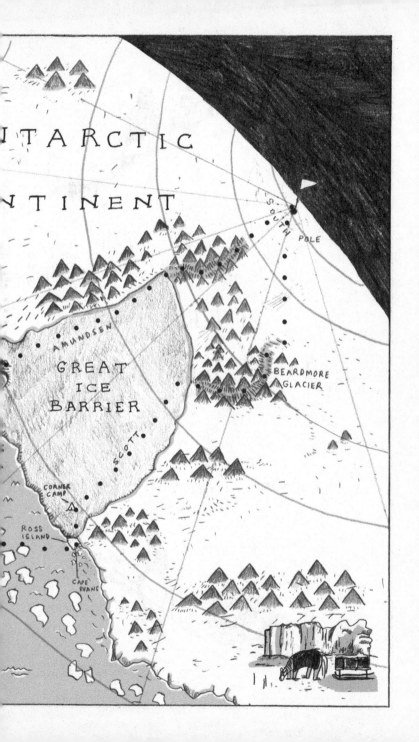

SITE OF
PONY CRISIS

GREAT

ICE BARRIER

SAFE
CAM

ROUTE TO
THE POLE

CORN
CAM

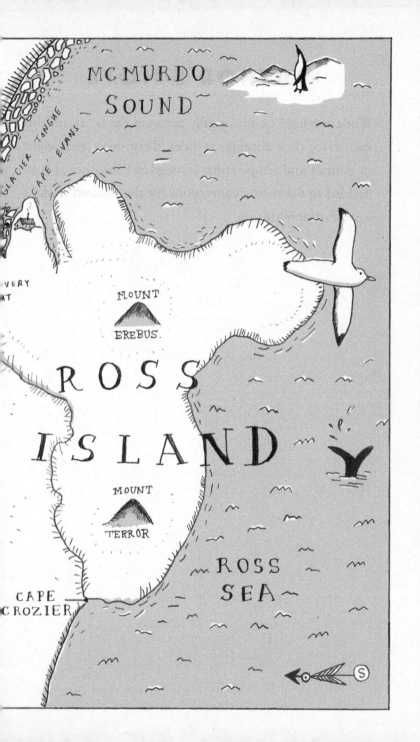

AUTHOR'S NOTE

While it would be historically accurate for Scott and his men to log their distances in miles, elevation in feet, weight in pounds and temperatures in degrees Fahrenheit, I have decided to use metric conversions for the modern reader's ease of comprehension.

If you're into happy endings, you'd better look elsewhere. This story does not end well. This is a story where men die, and their dreams of greatness die with them. But it is a fine story and one that is worth telling, from heroic beginning to tragic end.

Robert Falcon Scott lost everything in March 1912 in a tent on the Ross Ice Shelf. With his friends dead at his side, Scott reflected on his failed mission to be first to reach the South Pole and his inability to lead a small group of men back to safety. His own death was a matter of hours away, but his name would live on for more than a hundred years.

Most people hear the name Robert Falcon Scott and think of him in that tent on the brink of death. Some consider him a fool, an arrogant and rigid Royal Navy captain who believed in doing things a particular way even when hardship was the result. At the time he was remembered as a tragic hero, a steadfast leader who faced his untimely end with the dignity of a true English gentleman. Nowadays we appreciate Scott's humanity, his curiosity and his eagerness to learn from others.

Scott can still fill a room today. People flock to photographic exhibitions and to auction houses where odd remnants of his ill-fated *Terra Nova* expedition are sold to the highest bidder. The story of Scott, of how he tried and died, is well known. But what of the *Terra Nova* expedition itself? Who can tell you of the daring and adventurous men who sailed south with Scott, their story of bravery, hardship, discovery and survival, and their love and admiration for their leader? As it turns out, not many.

This is the story of the *Terra Nova* expedition and the memorable characters who, with a band of shaggy ponies and savage dogs, followed a man they trusted into the unknown.

CHAPTER ONE

SOUTHERN PACIFIC OCEAN – DECEMBER 1910

Herbert Ponting groans. It's not easy developing photographs on board a ship that is rolling up and down like a fairground ride. The ocean swell has been building in size for several hours but it's the added side-to-side motion that the photographer finds so difficult to stomach. The photographic chemicals slosh about in the developing baths. Thankfully the small table is bolted to the floorboards. Gripping the edge of it, Ponting steadies himself and squeezes his eyes shut. Try as he might, he can't block the fearful sound of the wind, howling through the rigging. He wonders how the sails will ever hold to the ship's masts. As keen as he is to continue in his task, he has to stop. Cupping his hand over his mouth, Ponting fumbles for the basin. Again, the stench of vomit fills the small cabin.

What madness drove him to sign up for this treacherous voyage to Antarctica? Ponting wishes himself back to New Zealand and the sunshine of Port Chalmers, where crowds of well-wishers jostled on the jetty. It was such a cheerful summer sight, with the flotilla of local boats bobbing about in the wake of the heavily laden *Terra Nova* as she made her way along the coast. That was a mere two days ago. And now this stomach-turning ordeal to endure.

Up on deck, the men take turns to pause in their duties and retch over the railing. They've long since emptied their guts but the seasickness gripping them all refuses to pass. It would be easy to curl into a ball and focus on feeling awful. Instead they follow their orders like good Royal Navy men without complaining – many of them have seen worse.

The sea is almost black. It heaves up and over the deck of the *Terra Nova* like an enormous animal eager for its supper. The horizon disappears as the ship plunges between two rollers. With the ship lurching up again, the men brace themselves for another wind-blown wave to slam into their side. At least keeping watch, tending to the animals and hauling sails can be done in the fresh air. The poor blighters shoveling coal in the engine room are sure to be surrounded by a right pong.

Down in the galley, the cook, Clissold, is preparing a meal that nobody will want to eat. He's feeling as ghastly as everybody else, and the smells of his own cooking in the windowless space are almost unbearable.

'Why am I even bothering?' he says loudly to the pots and pans that clash together every time the ship grinds up a wave and down the other side.

After the years he's spent at sea, Clissold still finds foul weather a trial. He feels hemmed in below decks, where every available space is packed tight with provisions. Boxes of biscuits and cans of meat and vegetables, a butter mountain, enough flour and sugar for an army, 162 frozen mutton carcasses, two whole frozen cows. Then there's all the other stuff loading the poor ship down – the pre-fabricated hut for their camp on the ice, 462 tonnes of coal, 3 tonnes of ice, enough paraffin to burn for a year, and crates upon crates of delicate scientific equipment. Clissold shakes his head when he thinks of everything that needs to stay afloat on the ocean. If only he could see what's happening outside, he might feel better. Or worse.

Scott peers out the porthole at the turbulent ocean. He misses his wife and son keenly, wondering why he's traded them for this mad caper. Kathleen. Little Peter. Dear little

Peter, who will have to celebrate two birthdays without his father. Scott knows that this sense of regret will pass. It did last time. Three years he was gone. But how beautiful his wife looked upon his return.

Thoughts of home must wait; Scott has more pressing issues demanding his attention. His clothes are still damp from the morning but he knows he'll be heading back up on deck again before too long so there's little point in changing. Besides the conditions are sure to get worse. Already the ocean looks confused, unsure of which way to turn. 'Dirty weather,' he mutters, squeezing into his clammy boots.

At sea since he was thirteen years old, Captain Scott can tell when something serious is brewing – even in his sleep. It's the heavy motion of the ship. He knows the *Terra Nova* is overloaded. Sitting low in the water and with a storm gathering, the ship is not in the best shape to ride out bad weather. He's already spent several hours with the bosun, inspecting the load on deck – among other things, there are nineteen ponies, thirty-three dogs, three motor sledges, twenty-nine sledges, countless sacks of coal and cases of petrol. They've done what they can to secure it all; now it's up to nature to show them the worst of her character.

Generally speaking, Scott is pleased with how well the *Terra Nova* has scrubbed up. Up until a few months ago, the wooden vessel was an old, dirty whaling ship that stank of blubber. But after a basic refit that used a fair share of the expedition funds supplied by company sponsors, the British public and the Royal Geographic Society, the ship is in good nick. Scott tries not to think of the leak. They've never been able to fix it completely. Then again, the *Terra Nova* has already made it to the ice and back, leak and all.

Up on deck a dog lifts its bedraggled head and lets out a long, anguished yowl. Wave after wave breaks across the side of the ship, swamping the Russian sled dogs, who shiver and roll themselves into ever tighter balls to try to escape the cold sea water. Meanwhile, the ponies fight to stay on their feet. Their hooves slide about on the slurry of vomit and manure that lines the floor of their cramped stalls as the ship pitches and rolls with increasing violence.

Scuttling across the exposed deck, holding on wherever they can, the men work under showers of sea spray. A number of coal sacks have worked themselves loose. Every time a wave hits the ship, the heavy sacks charge like battering rams across the deck and knock free whatever cargo they slam into. Thankfully nobody has yet been hit.

'The captain says he wants them thrown overboard!' the bosun shouts to the men.

'Overboard?'

'We've only just loaded them.'

'But we've got no way of getting any more, sir!'

'Get to work!' yells the bosun through the wind. 'The ship's overloaded.'

Steely blue water surges over the side. It swirls around the men's waists, threatening to drag them overboard along with any cargo that has worked loose. Working when they can, holding fast when they can't, the men send 10 tonnes of precious coal to the bottom of the sea. And with each sack they heave into the waves, they wonder if they'll have enough coal left to get back to New Zealand.

A howl, a flash of fur. A dog disappears overboard. Its chain breaks instantly as it is swallowed by a great swell.

'Did you see that?' The men stare, horrified, imagining the same happening to them.

'He's gone, that one,' the bosun says, leaning over to check.

'No, he's not!' Someone points as the next wave carries the same dog back onto the deck, sodden and scrambling for cover.

'Captain, we've got a problem,' says Lieutenant Evans, Scott's second-in-command. 'Too much water is coming over the sides. The deck's leaking. We're getting water-logged below.'

Scott scowls into the wind. 'This is turning into a nightmare. I want a full report of what's happening below.'

The report from the engine room is far from good. Lashly, the chief stoker, is neck-deep in sea water. Diving under repeatedly, he struggles to unblock the bilge pumps; they're so choked up with oil and engine-room sludge that they can no longer keep up with the rising water. He's been at it all day. He continues his frantic task until the boiler makes the sea water too hot to stay immersed in. Finally, towards midnight, Lashly abandons all hope of getting the pumps working. He knows sinking is a very real prospect.

A shout rings out. 'All hands below!'

Men run from all corners. Others tumble from their bunks. Sleep is the last thing on their minds with the storm at its most furious. The men grab buckets, pots, crates, canvas bags – anything they can use to bail out the ship. If they cannot control the level of the water, they'll all be dragged to the depths.

The icy wash from the deck tumbles onto the heads of the men below as they pass the buckets endlessly upward. Deep in the filthy bilge water, they forget their seasickness and sing shanties to focus their movements. The hours collapse under the weight of their task. Night passes into day and still they grind away, the buckets getting heavier and heavier and heavier. Their shoulders burn with the effort; their arms shake like rubber, but they have no choice. Exhausted is better than dead.

Then, slowly, a change in the tug-of-war – finally man is winning against nature. The water level in the engine room is showing signs of dropping at last.

'I've got an update, sir,' says Evans, braving the elements to communicate their first bit of good news to Captain Scott, who has been braced at the helm for longer than he cares to consider. 'Lashly's got the pumps working again!'

'Thank goodness,' says Scott. 'I thought the ship was handling better. With any luck we'll get under sail again soon.'

When the first light of dawn colours the eastern horizon, Scott makes his way along the upper deck. After three long days the sea is still mountainously high, but the wind has settled and there are breaks appearing in the cloud. Like everyone else aboard the *Terra Nova*, Scott is utterly spent. Sleep, for so many days an impossibility, now appears a blissfully anticipated luxury. Just knowing that his berth awaits is enough to keep the captain alert through his final rounds of the ship, appraising the damage and losses sustained during the storm. Two ponies lie dead in the stalls. A dog hangs limp and lifeless from its chain. But against all odds, Scott's men have won against nature's foul temper.

Back in his cabin, Scott sits in front of his diary, his pen poised above the page. What impressions will he record of the last few days? As he considers the seas rising higher than

8

ever, the devastating scene on deck, the fearful situation below in the engine room, Scott's thoughts instead turn to his men. He's never known such a good team. Officers and ratings – tireless workers every single one. As frightful as it was, Scott knows the storm has brought them together, encouraging a shared sense of purpose that would normally take weeks to foster. Exhausted, relieved, the men now know they can rely on each other no matter how dire their prospects.

CHAPTER TWO

Titus Oates cradles the pony's muzzle. 'You poor beast,' he says. 'Look at your poor swollen legs. You haven't a clue what's happening, do you?'

At least the dogs can lie down. They bury their snouts in their long shaggy coats and ignore the unpleasantness of their surroundings.

'It can't be much fun spending the whole sea journey on your feet,' says Taff, a beefy Welshman who was almost left in New Zealand after a drunken stumble off the gangplank into the water.

The pony's head bobs as if in agreement. In truth it's

the rhythm of the waves that moves the animal's head up and down, hour after hour, day after day.

Oates hasn't left the ponies once during the three-day storm. He can't interest them in eating or drinking. As miserable as they look now, Oates knows they'll look even more weak and forlorn before they make it to firm land. He knows about horses. He's a cavalry man, a war hero who earned himself the nickname 'No Surrender Oates'. As much as he loves horses, Oates is less than impressed by the ponies that have been selected for this important expedition. He's told the captain as much.

'They are the greatest lot of crocks I have ever seen,' he grumbled to Scott on first seeing them in Port Chalmers. 'The whole lot of them are totally unfit for any kind of work.'

Scott has wondered a few times if it was a mistake to accept the thousand-pound donation Oates paid to join the expedition. While he's already proved himself to be a hardworking, dependable sort during the storm, Oates certainly doesn't hold back with his comments – and he hasn't stopped complaining about Meares and his choice of ponies.

Poor old Cecil Meares. As the member of the expedition in charge of the dogs, he had no clue about ponies. Scott's advice was to buy only white ones, based on the fact that the majority of the Manchurian ponies that died during Ernest Shackleton's Antarctic expedition were dark in colour.

It may not be scientific but it's worth noting. Consequently the ponies Meares has purchased are a sorry bunch of nags, most of them better suited for boiling down for glue than hauling vital provisions to the South Pole.

The men, by contrast, are a cheery bunch, singing all day long, joking and roughhousing with each other on deck as the *Terra Nova* continues her journey southward. Scott is pleased with the interesting collection of individuals he's pulled together for the expedition. Navy men, scientists, doctors, engineers, a ski instructor, a cook, a photographer, a couple of Russian dog handlers and one rather wealthy paying customer with extremely bad eyesight and no training in anything other than history. With little existing expertise, Apsley Cherry-Garrard has been appointed assistant zoologist. He may be as blind as a bat but hopefully he'll be a quick learner.

With the storm behind them and the first icebergs looming on the horizon, Dr Wilson, the expedition's chief scientist, is delighted to have something other than endless sea to train his binoculars on. The men are all very fond of Dr Wilson and call him Uncle Bill. They know he's endlessly curious and point out any sight they think might hold interest for him.

'Thar she blows, Uncle Bill!' calls the lookout atop the mast.

Wilson puts down his binoculars. Just ahead, the blue-grey back of a whale breaks through the ocean's surface and shoots a spray of water from its blowhole. A week into their journey and sightings of the massive creatures have become almost commonplace.

'Never get sick of seeing that, do you, Uncle Bill?' says Lieutenant Bowers. 'Though it's a shame to be at such a distance. I'd like to get up closer.'

'Oh no, Bowers,' the scientist laughs. 'Any closer and you'll be covered head to toe in sickening fishy foulness every time one of them blows.' He wrinkles his nose. 'Believe me, not at all pleasant.'

'Speaking of unpleasant,' says Bowers. 'Have you heard about the leak in the men's sleeping quarters?'

'Oh dear. Is it serious?'

'Well, it's seriously smelly,' says Bowers, who's known as 'Birdie' on account of his small stature and beaky nose. 'It's a leak from the pony stalls. A sloppy mix of pony waste. The worse kind. It's been dripping through the decking and into the men's hammocks.'

'Good grief,' says Wilson. 'Does the captain know?'

'They don't want to bother the captain,' says Bowers. 'They've fixed it themselves. Rigged up a system of oilskins and canvas to deal with the worst of it. Drips off harmlessly to the side. The bedding stays dry, even if the air smells like a filthy stable.'

'Being waterlogged is miserable enough. But at least sea water doesn't smell rank,' says Dr Wilson. 'I'll never complain about going to bed in damp clothing ever again.'

This is the second time Wilson has made the journey to Antarctica. The first time was with Scott on his *Discovery* expedition in 1902. Having spent two whole winters there after their ship, the *Discovery*, became icebound, Wilson never thought he'd be so excited to be returning. It's a first for Birdie Bowers, though, and he's eager to prove himself a valuable addition to Scott's team.

In total, sixty-five men have set sail from New Zealand aboard the *Terra Nova*. Only thirty-three will stay with Scott to winter over on the ice before a smaller group will attempt to reach the pole in November, at the very beginning of the summer.

Once the supplies are unloaded from the *Terra Nova*, the ship will need to set off quickly to avoid becoming frozen in the pack ice. It would be bad enough to be stuck for a year without enough food for sixty-five men, but the prospect of the ship being crushed and sinking is even worse. With no way to communicate their situation to the outside world, the men would be stranded in Antarctica, with rescue a long time coming.

CHAPTER THREE

It's midnight. The sun dips briefly below the field of view. A rosy half-light makes the icebergs glow a faded green. An hour later the sun swells over the horizon and resumes its journey across the sky. Such is the southern summer night.

The *Terra Nova* steams on among the loose sheets of sea ice, picking a trail through the narrow 'leads' that allow the ship to pass without too much trouble. But it is still early summer and conditions are too good to last. After a few days it becomes impossible for the ship to keep a straight course. The thin sheets of ice are now forming into a more solid mass – they've hit the pack.

'There's been a fair bit of zigzagging lately, Captain,' says Ponting. 'Anyone would think we'd decided against heading south.'

'We must find ice that is still weak enough for the ship to push through. If we can't push the floes aside, we must go round them.'

'And what if there is no way forward at all?' asks Ponting.

Scott senses the photographer's unease, recognises the anxiety of a newcomer. He had similar misgivings the first time he ventured into sea ice. 'Don't worry Ponting. Give it a few hours and a small lead will mysteriously open up for us. We just need patience. Wind, sea currents, pressure from other ice – they all lend us a hand.'

The sea ice rises and falls on the ocean swell like a living, breathing thing. Some is young and slushy, little more than frozen foam. The older ice, already several seasons on the sea, has never floated far enough north to fully melt. It is thick and hard and sits on the water with all the permanence of giant flat islands. Every now and then huge pressure ridges rise up where two islands have forced themselves together in a violent, slow-motion embrace.

Ponting is hard at work taking photos of these craggy ice castles. Everywhere he looks he sees wonderful colours and visual effects. But capturing them on his black-and-white film is a tricky business. He'll need a lot more practice to get the most out of his photographic equipment in an environment so awash with light.

The voyage south turns into a waiting game. For hours the ship remains wedged in, without an obvious route forward. Sometimes the hours turn into days. While they wait, some of the crew help the scientific team. They check the depth of the ocean by lowering a weight on a line until it hits the bottom. Others monitor water temperature or draw samples from the sea floor. All of it is new information.

When the ice appears thick enough, some venture over the side of the ship to get a spot of exercise. Oates and Bowers follow the Norwegian ski master, Gran, across the ice on skis to investigate what looks like an island on the horizon. It turns out to be nothing but a colossal iceberg, but at least they've started on their much-needed skiing lessons.

The ice offers the crew a wonderful supply of fresh water. The Welshman, Taff, is off ship, sawing away. Broad shouldered, he has little trouble heaving the solid blocks up and onto a wooden platform to be winched aboard.

The sea ice also delivers a new source of food. The basking crabeater seals stare up at the ship with their round, beetle-black eyes. Blinking, interested, they're not at all scared of the looming bulk of the *Terra Nova* or the men massed by the railings. Neither are they scared of the rifle that one man has raised to his shoulder.

'Livers for supper tonight, chaps,' beams the cook. 'They might be a touch fishier than what you're used to at home, but I can guarantee they'll be entirely delicious.'

When it's clear that the ship is resolutely stuck, Captain Scott gives the order to put out the engine fires. Silence settles on the *Terra Nova*.

The sun is beating down. The glare from the pack ice is blinding. Everyone is now wearing goggles. Gran has taken more of the men off the ship for skiing lessons. It's completely new for most of them and they laugh at the strange gliding sensation. A few, including Scott, practise pulling each other along on skis to see how they'll manage hauling sledges.

'You're looking good, sir,' says Gran in his singsong Scandinavian accent.

'It feels great to get some decent exercise,' says Scott, a little short of breath. 'And by the looks of it, we're not the only ones to benefit from stretching our legs.'

Meares organises a sledge to be lowered over the side. He harnesses up fourteen of the fattest dogs to pull it and is now running wide rings around the ship, whooping loudly with delight. Puffing and panting, the dogs are clearly enjoying their first physical workout after weeks of lying around, snapping at each other.

'All right for some,' says Oates, leaning on the ship's

railing. 'What those wretched ponies wouldn't do for a little frolic on the ice.'

'And I'd like to try out my motor sledges, for what it's worth,' says Lashly. The chief stoker is a no-nonsense sort who likes to be busy. Lazing around doing very little is not his style. He wrinkles his nose at the smoke drifting his way from Oates's pipe and waves it away. 'For all the money those motor sledges cost Captain Scott, it would be good to actually see if they work.'

Days stretch into nights. Without darkness to mark the passing of time, the men feel slightly detached from reality. Stuck tight, the *Terra Nova* has no option but to drift north with the ice. It's not a good feeling to be heading back in the direction they've come from, but everyone is hopeful a lead will eventually open up and they can recommence their southern journey.

They've been ten days in the pack, five of them utterly stalled. At his desk, Scott unscrews his fountain pen and begins the messy job of filling it with ink. He marks Monday 19 December in his diary. Just what they needed, a couple of good days under their belt with some definite forward progress. They managed to set sail on the foremast and push slowly through the lighter floes for several hours at a time. Even so, Scott remains cautious.

Sure enough, the following day their advance is halted again.

'What an exasperating game this is, Evans!' says Scott to his second-in-command as they survey the solid white mass before them. 'It's impossible to tell what's going to happen. One moment everything looks great, next minute we're stuck fast.'

Evans agrees. He knows the delays are weighing heavy on their leader and on the morale of the men. They still have an awfully long way to go. Once they reach Antarctica, the unloading could take a good few weeks. They won't be able to see the *Terra Nova* safely off again until they've assembled their camp – the men's sleeping quarters, a communal space, rudimentary laboratories, a sanitation block, as well as some shelter for the ponies and dogs. But if the *Terra Nova* doesn't get away safely to open water . . . what then?

Scott rubs his temples. He hadn't bargained on the *Terra Nova* becoming wedged in the ice floes on the voyage down. It hadn't been like this on his first voyage south. Then again, the *Discovery* had left later in the summer season, when more of the sea ice had melted.

Being forced to drift for weeks away from the destination could endanger the whole expedition before it even begins. Another concern is the condition of the animals – the wretched ponies, forced to stand in their stalls for weeks with no meaningful exercise. They're getting visibly weaker as each day passes. This morning one collapsed in its stall the very moment Scott was passing by. Oates and a few others had struggled to get the creature back on its feet. For once Oates had held his tongue. No words were necessary. Scott had known from the look on his face exactly what the cavalry man was thinking.

CHAPTER FOUR

Dr Wilson is out on the ice. He's singing. And he has an audience. Not only the crowd of men lounging about on the deck of the *Terra Nova*, but also a large gathering of Adélie penguins. The louder he sings, the closer they come. Waddling over towards Uncle Bill, the curious birds appear like a legion of tiny tenors in black-and-white tuxedos, ready to join in.

'*God save our gracious King . . .*' drones Meares from the railing with a grin. A few of the dogs start to howl. Terrified, the penguins scurry for the nearest patch of open water.

Wilson scowls up at the laughing crew. 'I really wish

you hadn't done that, Meares. It'll take me another hour to tempt them back. I was rather hoping to catch one of them as a specimen.'

'I wonder,' whispers Clissold to Lashly. 'A penguin breast entrée just might be a festive addition to the Christmas table.'

Lashly looks horrified. He knows Clissold is probably not joking.

Icebergs come and go. Locked in the ice much like the *Terra Nova*, the bergs must go wherever the sea current takes them. Scott paces up and down, appraising the situation whenever a berg looms too close to the vessel.

'They're beautiful square things, are they not?' says Ponting, adjusting his camera tripod to capture the full majesty of the ice wall slowly approaching on the starboard side. 'And massive. Some are literally as tall as a building.'

'Indeed,' Scott says. 'You don't want to be caught between one of these beauties and an immoveable floe.'

To be slowly crushed in an icy vice is but one hazard. Scott doesn't care to mention his other concern – that the side of one of these giants could sheer off at any moment, smashing a hole in the hull and killing anyone unlucky enough to be under its tremendous weight.

'Vigilance, men,' Scott reminds the crew. 'Remember it will take us a good two hours to get the coal fires up to temperature and producing enough steam to get us moving out of harm's way –so keep your wits about you. You especially, Birdie. Keep your eyes peeled for any possible danger.'

'Right you are, Captain.'

Birdie Bowers has shown a real talent for picking when the ship can break through the ice and when they shouldn't bother. He often takes the helm, driving the *Terra Nova* full throttle at the ice, ramming the bow into the thick white sheets. Sometimes his strategy works, sometimes the ship simply rises out of the water and, with a horrifying crunch, cleaves back into the ice. It's slow going and more often than not, Bowers has to reverse and take a few more runs at it. Black coal smoke billows from the smoke stack at the back of the ship and leaves a faint grey track on the ice behind them.

The state of the coal reserves is yet another worry for Scott.

'How much do we have left, Lashly?'

'Less than 300 tonnes, sir,' says Lashly in a matter-of-fact fashion, his voice echoing in the silence of the engine room.

'This ship simply eats coal,' says Scott wearily. 'I'm worried that we'll remain stuck in the ice until Christmas at the soonest. I know what I'll be asking Saint Nick for – any sign of black water.'

Lashly clears his throat. 'Losing those 10 tonnes in the storm didn't help. We'll need every little bit of coal left if we're to make it all the way south, then get these boys home again.'

Every time the ship gets properly stuck, Scott gives the order for the fires to burn out. It's a waste of coal, but to keep the fires burning when there is no hope of making forward progress is even more of a waste. Getting the fires back up to temperature takes even more coal – the whole situation poses a horrible dilemma for poor old Scott. One he didn't anticipate.

CHAPTER FIVE

'Farewell to the pack ice!' shouts Ponting to nobody in particular.

After twenty days of feeling utterly trapped, the photographer is relishing the feeling of wind on his face as the *Terra Nova* cleaves through the waves. Mountains rise from the dark line of the horizon. It's a promising sight on New Year's Eve with only two hours remaining of 1910.

Landing the shore party is something that has been occupying Scott's mind for some time. He's discussed his plan with his second-in-command.

'Cape Crozier, on the eastern shore of Ross Island, has

a lot to offer, Evans. Comfortable quarters for the hut, ice for fresh water, snow for the animals, good slopes for skiing, vast expanses of rock for walks. Proximity to the Barrier and to the rookeries of two types of penguins, easy ascent of Mt Terror, good ground for biological work, good peaks for observation of all sorts, fairly easy approach to the Southern Road, with no chance of being cut off, and so forth . . .' he hesitates. 'There's only one problem.'

'What's that, sir?' asks Evans.

Scott gives a faint smile. 'I'm not entirely sure we can get ashore.'

There's a fearsome ocean swell when Scott, Evans, Oates and Cherry-Garrard are lowered over the side of the *Terra Nova* in a small boat to go and inspect a possible landing at Cape Crozier. As they get closer to the shore, they realise it's impossible to land men and equipment safely. They stare up at the high ice cliffs and the crevasse-riddled slopes beyond.

'Look at the penguins peering down at us from their nesting grounds,' laughs Cherry-Garrard, taking to his new role of assistant zoologist with enthusiasm.

'You'd do better to look down here,' says Oates, indicating the dark shadow of a killer whale circling lazily beneath their boat.

Scott notices the worried look on Cherry's face. 'What an excellent time these animals must have with thousands of penguins passing to and fro. There's no hunger here, my friend.'

'And clearly no safe place to land either,' says Evans drearily.

The *Terra Nova* presses on further west around Ross Island, which is fixed firmly to the mainland by a barrier of ice the size of France. It's an area Scott knows well from his first visit. Rounding Cape Bird, the northernmost point of the island, and heading up McMurdo Sound, Scott feels a warm excitement take hold, almost like he's coming home after a long absence. Back in 1901, his *Discovery* expedition had based itself at the extreme edge of Ross Island. Hut Point, as they called it, at the end of McMurdo Sound.

The *Terra Nova* glides through the slushy ice of McMurdo and slows as it approaches the hard bay ice two and a half kilometres from the shore. Scott, Wilson and Evans walk across the ice to take a closer look. Frozen to the coast, this sea ice will provide a sturdy platform to unload the ship onto. It's perfect.

'Let's call it Cape Evans,' Scott says, 'in honour of our excellent second-in-command.' It seems the right thing to do.

Back on board, Taff and Lashly, who were both part of Scott's earlier *Discovery* expedition, look out at the rocky shore with its irregular patches of snow. Beyond rises the familiar volcanic cone of Mt Erebus. They're unlikely friends: Taff, who likes nothing more than a drink and a smoke, and Lashly, who can think of nothing worse.

'Good to be back,' says Taff with a grin.

'Funny how you can't wait to leave this place and yet once you're gone, you'll do anything to return,' says Lashly.

For both men, it will be home for the next twenty-two months. For one of them, it will be the last home he'll ever know.

CHAPTER SIX

Skinny, sickly and suffering from an itchy skin condition, the ponies are a tragic sight. As much as they've suffered during their month-long sea voyage, they're now reluctant to leave their stalls. One by one, they're manhandled, cajoled and tricked into a narrow horse box and lifted over the side of the *Terra Nova* and onto the ice. Oates is exhausted with the effort, but seeing the ponies kicking up their hooves and rolling for joy on the ice lifts his spirits to the point where he'd like to do the same.

The dogs are enjoying freedom as well, although of a different sort. Meares has put them to work almost immediately, ferrying heavy loads to the shore. Suddenly there is noise and action and excitement in the vast white landscape. The sudden burst of activity has brought out crowds of penguins, keen to investigate the unfolding scene like nosy neighbours.

'Look at them waddle forward,' says Scott. 'They're so absurd. They don't seem to care that there's a string of howling dogs desperate to get at them.'

'Madness,' Wilson replies as the line of penguins advances. 'They're not daunted in the least.'

'Yes, their ruffs go up and they squawk but they don't back away. Nothing stops them. Not even when the men try to head them off.' Scott sighs. 'Oh dear, look at that . . .'

A dog has finally got hold of one of them. There's a shrill cry, then a red patch on the snow. Still the birds linger, a squawking, jostling crowd.

The penguins aren't the only locals coming for a closer look. A group of killer whales skirt the edge of the ice, assessing their prospects for a feed. There are six or seven of them. Noiselessly they slide their snouts above the waterline and eye a couple of dogs tethered by the edge.

'Ponting!' Scott calls too late. The glistening heads disappear before Ponting can snap them.

Ponting has spent all morning documenting the unloading of the ship. He's keen for some wildlife. He dashes over to the dogs, his camera at the ready. It should be a good shot.

'Can anyone see where they went?' he shouts.

There's a boom. The ice explodes under Ponting. A dozen loose pieces rock wildly as the whales send shockwaves through the water to unsettle their prey. The dogs howl, their claws scrabbling madly on the ice. Ponting clings to his tripod. With wide eyes and his mouth set in a terrified grimace, he leaps to safety.

One by one, the whales' heads pop up to survey their scene of destruction. Their mouths full of sharp white teeth, they seem to be laughing at the commotion they've caused.

'Oh, good gracious me,' Ponting looks about wildly, as if expecting the whales to hit again.

'You're a lucky man,' Wilson steadies the photographer, sitting him down on a crate of hot chocolate.

Scott's own heart is racing. 'I think we've all learnt a valuable lesson. Everyone needs to keep well clear of the edge.'

'I never thought it possible,' says Ponting, his face drained of colour. 'The ice over there, it's a good two and a half feet deep.'

'I know killer whales would snap up anyone in the water. But I've never seen them act with such deliberate cunning. Did you see how they were able to break that thick slab of ice? And acting together like that . . .' Scott shakes his head. 'They're such smart creatures. I think we'll need to treat them with more respect in future.'

'You can see why they're called the wolves of the sea,' says Wilson. 'By the way, I trust you got the shot?'

'No, I did not,' Ponting says, laughing. 'It looks like I shall have to put myself on the line again.'

Two of the three motor sledges are up and running, hauling goods ashore. Considering how much sea water washed over them during the storm, it's amazing that they're still in working order. The motor sledges are considered one of the expedition's secret weapons; they're by far the most expensive.

'Three motors at a thousand pounds each, nineteen ponies at five pounds each, thirty-two dogs at thirty shillings each,' Oates comments loudly to the huddle of men admiring the motor sledges. 'If Scott fails to get to the pole he jolly well deserves it.'

After several days, the task of unloading the ship is progressing as efficiently as can be expected. The ponies and dogs have been working hard and the motor sledges are being put through their paces too. Even the men have harnessed themselves up and are dragging sledges heavy with equipment, petrol, oil, canned food and building supplies. Anyone not busy hauling has been hard at work on shore, organising provisions and erecting the hut where the thirty-three-strong shore party will sleep, eat, cook, work and entertain themselves throughout the long dark Antarctic winter.

It's the second time the hut has been erected. The first time was back in New Zealand, before the *Terra Nova* set sail. Once everything was checked, it had been carefully packed away again to ensure no important components were missing. Many sections of the hut have been pre-fabricated but, even so, fitting them all together offers the men a giant puzzle.

'What will keep us all warm?' asks one of the carpenters, pointing to the large gaps between the planks making up the walls.

'We've got a big stove to heat the interior of the hut,' says Birdie Bowers, whose excellent organisational skills have been put to good use. 'But we'll also get the men to pack the walls with sacking filled with seaweed to insulate us from the winds. And Scott has suggested we pack the pony fodder around the outside of the hut to add another buffer layer.'

Out by the ship, a pony's leg goes through the ice. It stumbles, shifts its weight and settles on firmer footing. Every now and then a pony takes fright and gallops away. The least thing sets them off. One gets spooked by its harness, capsizes its load and bolts for shore with its ears back and its eyes bulging. Oates walks after it and once the animal has come to its senses and halted its mad dash he calmly leads it back to the ship, speaking soothing words all the way. If these creatures are to be any use to the expedition, they must get used to pulling sledges through snow and ice, harnesses and all.

The dogs, too, have moments of skittishness. One sledge team flies away at breakneck speed. One dog is caught off guard and is dragged for almost half a kilometre before it can get in step with the rest of the team. There are two Russian dog handlers, Anton and Dimitri, but Meares is the one ultimately in charge of the dogs. Among other specialised skills needed to run the teams, Meares has to learn Russian, not only to communicate with the handlers but to issue commands to the dogs as they work.

Ponting is still learning, too. He finds everything about his new environment visually stunning. 'This is the most beautiful spot I have ever seen – I need all day and most of the night to gather it all in,' he declares. While the others set about organising the camp, Ponting casts out on his own across the floes, hauling a sledge full of heavy photographic equipment in the hope of capturing more and more spectacular shots of the ice.

'Will you look at that,' he says to himself, focusing on yet another remarkable sight in the distance. He readies his camera. There's an odd sensation. Water pools at his feet. He and his heavy sledge are sinking.

Ponting lunges forward. He gives it everything he's got. Each footstep disappears under the ice but he's got just enough purchase to take another, then another, then another frantic step. He's running on water. When his boots finally connect with something solid, he dashes like a headless chicken for another fifty metres. Panting, pink and sweating through multiple layers of clothing, Ponting collapses onto his knees.

'Two lucky escapes in as many days,' he breathes. 'How on earth will I survive the year?'

CHAPTER SEVEN

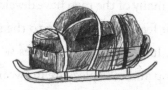

'I'm actually sunburnt.' Titus Oates stares at his arms, bare from the elbows down. 'Here I am surrounded by white and I'm slowly turning red.' Cuts and abrasions cover his hands from hefting boxes, hauling ropes and buckling and unbuckling pony harnesses. But he's used to blood and he doesn't mind hard work. In fact, it's what he likes.

'It's my eyes that hurt the most,' Taff says, licking his lips again even though he knows he shouldn't. They're horribly cracked and sore from the sun and dry air. 'Bright light bouncing off the ice – you can't get away from it. Look up, you're blinded, look down, you're blinded. Close your eyes and you're still blinded. I can't wait to get indoors and rest my eyeballs.'

Oates gives the Welshman a good-natured shove. 'Stop your complaining. I don't need your eyeballs, I need your big strong arms. Bring them over here.'

After the days of unloading the ship, there's a whole symphony of ills to share. As well as sunburn, sore lips and snow blindness, many of the men have developed blisters on the soles of their feet from trudging to the shore and back on the hard ice. It's easy to tell the ones who are affected. They hobble, limp and take pleasure in swearing. As long as it's out of Scott's earshot. The captain is a navy man, but he can't abide bad language.

The intense sun is having an effect on the ice too. It's clearly deteriorating. Using long sledges, the men can still cross any slushy patches by running at speed and allowing the sledges' momentum to carry them. But landing the remaining cargo safely will become more and more difficult. There's not much more to unload but assuming the fine weather continues, everyone will need to work a little faster.

'Let's get that last motor sledge onto the ice,' calls Scott. 'If we can get it working with the other two alongside the ponies and dog teams, that'll speed things up.'

Lashly organises a team of the strongest men to lower the third and last of the heavy machines over the side. One of them has just taken hold of the pulley rope when his body drops straight through the ice. His shoulders wedge him in place but if he should slip below, he won't get out. He flails for a handhold. The others run to his aid. Hauling him to safety, the men hear a strange creaking noise. The motor sledge tips slightly. The ice is giving under its weight.

'Grab the rope, lads!' Lashly yells.

The machine dips further to one side, then suddenly disappears. The rope snakes away at speed but not before four men manage to grab it, their bare hands taking the strain.

'Hold her steady,' Lashly says, not wanting to take his eyes from the unfolding scene.

Pulled taut, the rope cuts like a knife through the ice towards the men. It's a dreadful choice facing them. Hold tight and be dragged below the surface or simply let go of one of the most expensive pieces of equipment on the expedition. There's much shouting. The dogs are barking. Men are grunting and turning red in the face. But the task is too great. One by one, they release the rope. A hole in the ice is all that remains. A few bubbles rise to the surface.

'There goes a thousand pounds,' Oates says.

Scott's head appears over the ship's railing. 'What's all the commotion?'

Lashly scratches the back of his head. He doesn't believe in beating about the bush so he just says it. 'The motor sledge has gone through the ice, sir.'

'What? There?' Scott points to the yawning gap in the ice.

'I'm sorry . . . we tried to stop it. But it's gone to the bottom, sir.'

Scott looks about. 'Everyone safe? Everyone accounted for?'

Lashly nods. 'Everyone accounted for.'

Scott slams his fist onto the railing. He's furious. Luckily, the captain's rage is directed at himself, at his own lack of foresight. 'I knew the ice was getting too thin . . . I just knew it!'

Lieutenant Evans appears at his shoulder. 'Sir, many heavy loads have crossed that same area without a hint of danger. We couldn't have foreseen this.'

'The motor sledge is nothing, it's gone. We can't do anything more about it.' Scott shakes his head. But such vital equipment. Such promising equipment. Scott takes a deep breath and counts to ten. 'Somebody will get seriously hurt if we're not more careful, Evans. We must finish unloading the supplies and equipment before conditions get even worse. Let's get more hands on deck. And Evans,' he says, 'make sure to take extreme care. I don't want to lose any men to those orcas.'

A few hours later a dark wedge of water has opened up and the men are completely cut off from the *Terra Nova*. Using semaphore flags to communicate, Scott signals the ship to move further north, where a safe spot has been found along the ice edge. They cannot afford to abandon the operation. Absolutely everything is needed off that ship.

Bowers has checked every case coming ashore against his manifest and stacked everything in the appropriate place. Forever bustling this way and that, Bowers has set himself a list of vital tasks. It seems impossible for the man to sit still.

Scott hasn't failed to notice Birdie's energy and dedication. 'Isn't Lieutenant Bowers an impressive fellow?' he comments to Dr Wilson. 'He knows at once where every case, every article of clothing or equipment is stashed. I have to admit, when I first saw him, I thought him a very odd specimen and quite unfit for our purposes. But he's one of the most capable, hardworking men I've ever come across. We're very lucky to have him.'

'Bowers, where's the tea?' Wilson calls out to him by way of a lighthearted test.

'Behind the piano, third box down on your left between the pony fodder and the cases of flour.'

'Are you sure about that, Birdie?' Keohane quips, keen to join in the joke.

'Yes,' says Bowers, continuing his bustling. 'Quite sure.'

The finishing touches are being made to the hut. Soon the men will be able to leave the tents they've pitched on the ice and settle into their permanent beds at Cape Evans. Not that they're expecting any great comfort or privacy in their new home. Scott, his officers and the scientific staff will each have a cubicle, but the rest will have to bunk down together. They don't mind the separation between officers and men. It's standard navy stuff. In any case, there'll be no pony effluent raining down on their heads like on board the *Terra Nova*.

The hut has been built in a nice sheltered spot on a beach of black lava. It is a little close to the shore for Scott's liking – only three and a half metres above the high tide mark – but there are no indications that the sea has ever reached this far up. Besides, the sea ice is sure to dampen any major storm swell. Now that the floor, roof and walls have been insulated from the winds, the hut is as weather tight as any hastily built home on the ice can be. If there are any improvements that can be made, Scott is sure this able collection of men will soon make them.

The same cannot be said for the pony quarters. While walls have been erected from stacked bales of hay, there are no materials of any kind left to make a roof. A tarpaulin will just have to do. The dogs don't even have that. Bedding down in the snow, they'll rely on thick fur alone for protection against the elements.

With everything going so well at Cape Evans, Scott and Meares take a dog team on a short trip towards Hut Point, where Scott's *Discovery* expedition set up a decade earlier. On the way they find an old supply depot. It's from Ernest Shackleton's team two years ago. Everything is perfectly preserved. Not so the old *Discovery* hut. It has obviously been used by Shackleton and his men, and left in terrible condition. A window has been forced open and the whole of the interior has filled with solid ice. It's impossible to get inside.

'It's so very disappointing, Meares,' says Scott. 'Such carelessness. These huts should be better looked after. They're for everyone to use. They're not just a temporary resource built for the members of a particular expedition – here today, gone tomorrow. Goodness knows, in this environment, we need all the shelter we can get.'

After a restless night in a tent, Scott and Meares spend the next morning looking around. Very little has changed in the last decade, including the wooden cross that overlooks the bay. The paint still looks fresh. It was erected after one of the *Discovery* crew, George Vince, became disorientated during a blizzard and stumbled over a cliff. The cross is a reminder that, amid all the excitement of settling into their new home, death is never far from view.

CHAPTER EIGHT

Now the organisation of the Cape Evans camp is complete, Scott starts to think about his next step: depot laying. January is fast disappearing and they must get away soon to make the most of what's left of the short summer season.

Supply depots will form the backbone of their polar mission. The South Pole lies more than 1200 kilometres away from Cape Evans. Hauling enough provisions for both the outward and homeward journey is not possible. They'll need to stash food, cooking fuel and other vital supplies along the way beforehand. Of course the depots they're planning to lay now won't reach the pole. They won't even reach halfway.

They simply don't have enough time – winter will soon be upon them. Further depots will need to be laid on the actual polar journey. The plan is for the sledges to get lighter as the effort required to haul them becomes ever greater.

The smell of baking bread fills the Cape Evans hut. Clissold squares his sore shoulders, pulls off his apron and joins the others talking in small groups in the dim light. *Cosy, that's what this is*, thinks the cook. *For the first time in a long while we're not cold, damp or soaked in sweat.*

Scott clears his throat. The room falls silent. Thirty-two eager faces turn from idle conversation with neighbours to listen to their leader outline his plans for the coming weeks.

'February days are long and the temperatures are still relatively mild. If we are to set out for the pole in early November, we'll need to have made all the necessary preparations to get us off on a good start in the next few weeks.'

There's murmuring, shifting chairs.

'I have spent some time going over the plan – how far we'll need to travel and how fast – so that no depot shall be spaced too far away from the last. Pemmican will be our principal food source while out on the ice. For those of you who have yet to try it, I should say that it is an acquired taste – one I trust you will come to really enjoy.'

Clissold the cook gives a shudder. He's thankful to be staying in the warmth and familiar surroundings of Cape

Evans and not heading out into the icy unknown. While the others are gone, he'll continue his culinary experiments with seal and penguin meat, dreaming up exciting new dishes using these questionable delicacies. As inventive as his meals are, Clissold knows they're far tastier than anything the work parties will be eating. Pemmican – dried meat crushed to powder and mixed with fat – is not everyone's ideal meal, but it will deliver what the men need to survive out in the harsh Antarctic environment: fat for energy and protein for strength. Eaten in chunks or boiled up with water for a sloppy soup, the pemmican will make a return to Cape Evans (and Clissold's mystery meat dishes) all the more joyful.

'As well as pemmican, the sledging rations will include sugar cubes, cocoa, tea, butter and dry biscuits, delivering an equivalent of 4200 calories per man,' continues Scott. 'But I must warn you, once we start hauling a fully loaded sledge ourselves, we will undoubtedly use significantly more energy – perhaps over 5500 calories. We won't be following a nice smooth road. The deep snow, humps and hollows and icy ridges we will have to haul across will prove some of the most challenging terrain you've encountered in your life – I guarantee it.'

'What about the ponies, sir?' somebody asks. 'Won't they be pulling our sledges?'

'For a time, at least. But once we head up the Beardmore Glacier, the surface will become too difficult for animals to navigate. Not so for men. Skis will help us bridge the crevasses – there will be many – and that's something ponies and dogs can't easily do.'

'Then it's to be a skiing trip, sir?' asks Bowers. He's unsure about this new fad. He'd far rather trust in his own two feet than set off with two heavy planks strapped to his ankles. He tried it out when the ship was locked in the pack ice and didn't like it one little bit. Awkward things.

'Yes indeed, Lieutenant Bowers. We shall all be on skis.'

'Very sporting,' jokes Cherry-Garrard. 'Rather pleasant I should think.'

Scott laughs without humour. 'Don't be fooled, Cherry. There will be nothing pleasant about the places we are going. We shall be met by blizzards, white-out conditions and the fierce winds sweeping down from the interior. We shall all be severely tested.'

Taff raises his hand and asks, 'How many men will make the journey to the pole, sir?'

'Not everyone, sadly,' says Scott. 'I imagine that I will need three or four of the ablest men for the final assault on the pole.'

'Who might that be?' asks Oates with a grin.

'I'm not sure yet, Titus. I've got some time up my sleeve before I need to make that difficult decision. Of course a great number of you will be setting out from Cape Evans. We need manpower and lots of it to drive the ponies and dog teams and to transport supplies up the Beardmore Glacier. But each team will eventually turn back, leaving only the polar party.

'As much as I would like all of you to participate in the final push, we can't have everyone continuing the journey to the end. We simply cannot haul enough food for so many. Or risk so many lives on what will be a highly treacherous march into the unknown.'

The room buzzes. Despite Scott's grim warning, every man hopes he'll be one of the few chosen to make the final journey to victory at the pole.

CHAPTER NINE

'How on earth are we going to get all this stuff out there?' Birdie Bowers straightens his back and grimaces. It's a long way south.

Having done such a great job of organising the Cape Evans stores, Bowers has been put in charge of making all the necessary arrangements for the depot-laying trip. Almost 2500 kilograms of equipment and provisions are stacked up outside the hut. Twelve men will go, leading eight ponies and twenty-six dogs. A few of them have experienced the Great Ice Barrier before, on Scott's *Discovery* expedition. But not one of them has undergone specialised training to prepare for the athletic ordeal ahead of them. They are all eager to get going, if a little out of shape.

Bowers must find a way to balance the incredible weight across ten sledges. He also has to work out what to leave at each depot. Surrounded by boxes of biscuits, pony fodder, ropes, shovels, lamps and candles, teetering towers of metal fuel canisters, tents and skis, Bowers has no time for any busybodies. He must concentrate. He shoos the other men away whenever anybody offers to help. He paces up and down. The task is driving him around the bend. At night, even his dreams are filled with boxes.

It is one of the most important tasks of his life. If he makes any mistakes in calculating daily rations, men could die. Without adequate food, survival is uncertain. But without fuel to melt snow for water, severe dehydration will quickly lead to death. As well, there needs to be enough fuel to provide three hot meals a day. Hot food will enable the men to meet the subzero conditions every morning and will restore warmth to their exhausted bodies at the end of a day. The daily rations are easy enough to work out, but how on earth will he calculate the kerosene that is needed to heat each man's allowance of food, water and tea over the course of several months? Bowers scratches his chin. It is indeed a headache.

'Hold it there, Birdie,' calls Ponting across the piles

of crates marked *Drinking Cocoa*. 'Beautiful! That'll keep Mister Cadbury happy.' Ponting needs a lot of photos for the expedition's sponsors. Many have provided provisions free of charge. Bowers plants one foot on a crate and strikes a dramatic pose, as if he alone hopes to conquer the pole.

'I hope you've got some room for photographic equipment,' says Ponting.

'You're coming too?' Bowers is horrified that he might have to start his calculations all over again.

'Good gracious no!' laughs Ponting. 'I'm sending the lot off with Scott. He'll be the one keeping the photographic record out there. I'm afraid I'm too soft to head out into the wilds. Besides, with all that flat white space I wouldn't know where to aim my camera. I like proper landscape – mountains, sea – with some frightening wildlife to bring it all alive.'

Oates is readying the ponies. He can see a definite improvement in their condition since the end of their voyage, but they're hardly the finest specimens. Pure pulling power they are not.

'You load of old nags,' Oates sighs. 'I'll be surprised if you last a week out there in the open.'

'You really are a cheerful old pessimist aren't you, Titus?' says Cherry-Garrard. 'The ponies will be fine. They just need to get into the swing of it.'

Oates is right; the ponies will be truly challenged by the cold, by the wind, by the bright light of a sun that never sets. The work will be gruelling.

'Have you packed your bag, Oates?' Cherry asks.

'My bag?'

'Bowers says we're each allowed to take five and a half kilos of personal belongings. Some extra clothing and foot-wear, a book, some tobacco, pencil and paper maybe.'

'How about a gun to shoot these rubbish ponies when they go lame?' Oates asks. 'Or a gun to shoot the halfwit that chose them.'

Cherry laughs. 'Honestly Oates. Meares knows dogs. He should never have been asked to choose ponies. He says he doesn't know the first thing about them.'

'I wasn't talking about Meares,' Oates mutters to himself. He has developed a real dislike of Captain Scott, who he continues to hold responsible for the dismal state of the animals. He thinks it's ludicrous to have chosen ponies according to the colour of their coats. A leader shouldn't be so set in his ways, so certain that his way is the only way. Arrogance is a quality Oates cannot abide and as he sees it, Scott has it in abundance. But he also realises that hiding his true feelings about their leader is for the best. Nobody needs to know.

'What are these things?' Cherry picks up a tangled mess of wire and bamboo.

52

'Snow shoes,' snorts Oates. 'For the ponies. Have you ever heard a more ridiculous thing in your life?'

'I guess we'll see them in action soon enough,' Cherry says, handing them carefully back to Oates.

Oates flings them into the corner. 'Not likely. Useless things. I won't take them. Besides, none of the ponies has learnt how to walk in them.'

Cherry shrugs, 'That's one less thing Birdie needs to find room for on the sledges. Perhaps I can sneak another book into my bag.'

As the day of departure draws near, the hut hums with the excitement of men getting ready. This is really it – the first step towards their epic journey, and the first time many of them will set foot on the Great Ice Barrier, the massive ice shelf that sits between them and the hard landmass of the Antarctic plateau. Locked in place above the sea, the ice is thick, almost a kilometre in some places. While there's no chance of falling through like on the sea ice, the men will need to keep their wits about them to avoid losing animals or sledges down crevasses, or plummeting to a hideous death themselves. Nobody wants to see another cross erected at Hut Point.

CHAPTER TEN

Panic. The sea ice is breaking up. It was to serve as their road south, a way to cross McMurdo Sound all the way to the Barrier edge. The ice in the northern reaches of the bay is already gone. To the south, what little sea ice remains, looks likely to float away. They must hurry. Perhaps only hours remain.

The ponies move with haste, not along the coast as planned but further inland, where they are led down a steep rocky slope and across the glacier. Beyond them a wide stretch of dark water has opened up. The rate of thaw has caught them all by surprise.

Bowers is the last to leave Cape Evans. He's a good few kilometres behind, and anxious that nothing vital has been forgotten. Half running to keep up with his pony, Bowers is dressed up in all his spare layers of clothing so as not to overburden the poor beast. He's sweltering. His face is red. Sweat drips off the end of his beaky nose.

'Wait for me, you silly pony,' he calls, trying to catch his breath. The pony ignores him.

The provisions for the trip, the dogs and all of the sledges have been loaded back aboard the *Terra Nova*. The ship is steaming ahead to the end of McMurdo Sound to meet up with the men and ponies. Once unloaded, the ship will have one last task before heading back to New Zealand – to drop First Officer Victor Campbell and six others at a more easterly location on a separate scientific assignment.

The ship moors off the Glacier Tongue, an ice platform jutting out into the bay. It will take them several days to relay the supplies to a temporary camp near Hut Point, where Bowers will again fiddle with balancing the weight between the sledges. Bowers needn't have worried about burdening his pony with a few extra clothes. From here on, each pony will need to haul 225 kilograms of supplies.

Up until now, the men have had rock and ice underfoot. Stepping out on the Barrier for the first time, the surface suddenly changes. Deep snow. It's far from good.

Despite this, Scott is pleased with the ponies. After the poor performance of the sled dogs he used during his *Discovery* expedition, he's not at all convinced that dogs, which are only capable of taking light loads, are the way to go. Besides, Shackleton reported great success over snow and ice with his hardy Manchurian ponies, give or take the odd one that dropped down dead.

'Look, Wilson,' says Scott. 'They're so steady on their feet. Stepping out briskly. They look almost cheerful following in each other's tracks.'

'Fine creatures,' Wilson agrees, although he has his doubts. He's far happier to be trotting along with the dog team.

Manchurian ponies should be used to working in snow, their stout legs pumping up and down in the soft drift. But some hours into the first day, the ponies are already struggling. While they are strong enough to haul the sledges, their small hooves sink even when the men barely leave footprints on the surface.

There's Punch and Uncle Bill, Michael and Weary Willy, Blossom, Guts, Nobby and James Pigg, plodding along in single file. Leading the ponies, the men can't chat among themselves, so instead speak words of encouragement to the animals, hum to themselves or get lost in thought as they march towards the southern horizon that never seems to get any closer.

The pony called James Pigg has already gone lame.

'Come on, lad,' encourages Keohane, 'you'll be getting to the pole.' It doesn't make a difference. The animal is spent and many of the others look close to giving up.

Meanwhile, the dogs have their own problems. Although they are light and trot easily over the snow, they're not so good at pulling the heavy loads. They're also unpredictable and easily distracted. Driving a dog team takes years of practice and Scott has limited experience. He knows *ki ki* for 'go right', *chui* for 'go left' and *esh to* for 'lie down'. But none of these commands help when his dog team sets off at high speed to chase a whale. Just when it looks like they'll plunge into the open water at the edge of the Barrier, Scott manages to stop. His heart is racing; his hands are shaking.

'Give me a steadfast pony any day,' he says to Dimitri, one of the Russian dog handlers, when he finally catches up. Dimitri is breathless. He's relieved the leader is still with them and not bobbing about in the water with the sledge on the bottom of the bay. Scott realises there's another advantage to men hauling their own supplies – unlike dogs, men generally follow commands.

Little changes as they trudge onward across the undulating surface of the great snowy plain. The sky is the colour of metal, the sun a bright smear. The crunch of footsteps, the soft tapping of the harnesses and the murmuring of men cajoling their ponies are the only sounds in a vast silence. Some way off, two triangular shapes break the monotony of the landscape. Scott blows his whistle to call a halt.

'What do you think they are?' asks Bowers.

'Shackleton's tents,' says Scott. 'He passed through here a couple of years ago. On his way south – to the pole.'

'How far did he get?' asks Bowers.

'A long way. Across the Great Ice Barrier. Up the Beardmore Glacier. Onto the summit plateau. And there he turned back. But not before reaching 88 degrees south.'

Bowers nods, 'Pretty good. But it's not 90 degrees south.'

Scott smiles. 'No, he left 90 degrees south for us.'

Scott and Shackleton have a long history. But they haven't seen each other in some time. Scott thinks back to when he, Shackleton and Wilson attempted to cross the Barrier the first time, in 1902. It hadn't ended well. The dogs were exhausted and unable to haul, and the men ended up harnessed to the sledge themselves, the starving dogs trailing behind, dying off one by one. And poor Shackleton. Scurvy got him. And badly too. Too weak to haul, Shackleton had to be dragged on the sledge by Scott and Wilson for part of the way home.

'Astounding, isn't it?' says Wilson to Scott. 'One tent ripped to shreds, the other in perfect condition. Even a half-finished meal lying there. It looks like Shackles himself might have just popped out to relieve himself.'

'This is good news,' says Scott. 'If these canvas tents can withstand the polar blast for two years, then our supply depots will easily withstand one long winter.'

They christen their first major depot 'Safety Camp'. Everyone agrees it's a safe distance from the Barrier edge, which is famous for falling away in massive chunks. A lot can happen on the Barrier in nine months. Nobody wants precious supplies to disappear into the sea.

'Men, we must make sure the depot can be easily seen – even in a white out,' says Scott. 'Anything we put here will be covered in snow, so I need you to build height into our structure. Let's make it tall and steady.'

Birdie Bowers pushes a long thin pole into the snow and the men stack the provisions and equipment around it. After several hours of arranging, they stand back to admire their efforts – a ramshackle pyramid with a black flag on top. It should be visible. On the flat Barrier it's possible to see fifteen to twenty kilometres into the distance, as long as the weather is clear and the wind is not blowing clouds of snow off the surface.

It's nice to shed some weight from the sledges. The ponies are struggling. Everyone has been caught off guard by the condition of the snow. They are not making the distances required to keep to their depot-laying schedule. The longer it takes, the less likely their own provisions will last and the more likely they are to dig into the depot supplies.

Anxious to speed things up, Scott tries a set of snow shoes on Weary Willy. They work a treat. Oates is amazed. Weary Willy can walk on the soft snow – no sinking at all. It's like he's on firm ground.

'Let's get them on all the ponies,' says Scott, thrilled at the success of the innovation.

'We won't be able to do that, sir,' says Oates.

'Why not?'

'I left them behind.'

'You left them behind?'

'I didn't think it worth the extra weight.'

'And now? Can you see now how that extra weight would have helped us?'

'Yes.' Oates's answer appears as a white cloud, a thick regretful breath.

'Somebody will have to go back for them.' Scott storms off – it seems unlikely that they will make any more progress today.

In the end, Meares and Wilson offer to head back to Cape Evans. It is 32 kilometres but the distance is worth it if the snow shoes can help pick up the pace. But it's bad news. The ice that they walked the ponies across barely a week ago has melted. They are cut off from Cape Evans completely.

They must press on, with Weary Willy blazing a trail and all the other ponies floundering far behind.

Oates is not the only member of the party that Scott is frustrated with. Atkinson, the expedition surgeon, can no longer keep quiet about his painfully blistered heel, which has rubbed raw in his new boots. After a couple of days he's limping badly and threatening to hold up the whole team.

Wilson examines the heel, 'It's no good,' he says to Scott. 'He'll have to stay here.'

'I cannot have much sympathy,' replies Scott. 'You ought to have reported his trouble long before.'

It's a blow for Atkinson, but worse for Tom Crean, who Scott orders to stay with the patient at Safety Camp. Atkinson and Crean watch the depot party move off from Safety Camp until they are specks on the horizon.

'How lonely they look,' says Atkinson. 'Heading off into the distance like that.'

'And how I wish I was there to keep them company,' sighs Crean.

CHAPTER ELEVEN

'Shut the flap!' the men shout in unison.

Oates blunders into the tent, a white figure with the blizzard bursting in about him. He's fed the ponies and secured their blankets as best he can against the onslaught of wind and snow. Meares and Wilson have attended to the dogs. Having consumed their chunks of frozen seal meat, the dogs are now nothing more than white mounds under a layer of fresh snow. The sledges have also disappeared under immense drifts. Safe in their tents, the men have supper and wish an end to the foul weather. They've already been cooped up for forty-eight hours.

Oates removes his fur mitts and his camel-hair helmet, and peels back his frozen balaclava, careful not to scatter his tent mates with loose snow. He removes his fur boots and his windproof outer shell. A jersey, flannel shirt and several layers of underclothing will serve as his pyjamas as he slips into his reindeer sleeping bag to sip sugary tea and down his thick pemmican stew.

'Your nose doesn't look good,' says Lieutenant Evans, licking his bowl clean.

'Well, it's still attached to my face at least,' laughs Oates, slurping his supper. 'Tell me when it falls off.'

There's not much they can do while confined to their tents by the blizzard. The temperature frequently dips below minus 20 degrees Celsius.

'And they call this summertime,' says Cherry-Garrard from the comfort of his sleeping bag.

'Funny kind of summer when you have to worry about frostbite rather than sunburn,' says Evans.

'Looks like I might have to worry about both,' says Oates, massaging some feeling back into his nose.

While they're moving, the men are able to stay warm. When they have to force a pony back to its feet or heave a sledge from deep snow, they get hot enough to break out in a sweat. But in the mornings, many are forced to stand still in the intense cold with their ponies while the stragglers get themselves organised. On such mornings, there are grumpy faces aplenty.

Overall progress is not good. With no snow shoes, perhaps it would be better to rest during the day and travel at night. While it doesn't get dark, the sun is lower in the sky and the slightly cooler temperatures make the surface firmer for the ponies. The dogs, on the other hand, bounce along over the deepest snow as if nothing is amiss. But hunger, hard work and the constant cold are starting to have an effect on their behaviour. They're turning more wolf-like every day. When food appears, their tempers flare and fights are all too frequent. One dog lashes out and grabs Scott by the leg, sinking its teeth through his pants. The dog retreats, snarling. Too close, Scott realises. He mustn't think of them in the same terms as one would a contented pet. These are fierce working dogs that cannot be approached in a casual manner. He won't make that mistake again. If they weren't still harnessed to the sledge, it's probable that all the dogs would have gone for him, leaving an almighty mess to clean up.

'Hunger and fear rule a dog's life,' he says as Wilson examines the wound. 'It doesn't take much for a quiet, peaceful team wagging their tails one moment to become a bunch of raging, tearing, fighting devils the next.'

'Luckily it's superficial, Robert,' says Wilson. 'Best to keep everyone clear of those dogs. Men and ponies alike. They're getting rather savage.'

The party trudges on, day after day, with no improvement in the hideously difficult conditions. Ponies get stuck, sledges tip over. The snow is so deep in parts that it becomes impossible to progress without ponies pulling and men pushing. Almost three weeks have passed since they left Cape Evans. They've struggled on, hoping the surface will improve. But if anything it's worse, especially after the three-day blizzard that kept them in the tents. Three supply depots have been laid. One final drop remains. Then they can turn around and head home.

The men coax the floundering ponies, all of them panting and heaving and half engulfed in snow. One pony collapses with the effort of freeing itself from a deep drift and is left trembling on the snow until it can regain its feet. Weary Willy in particular is suffering. Weak, and slower than the others, he cannot keep pace with the main group, even with the snow shoes on. The Norwegian ski master, Gran, does his best to keep Weary Willy going, but they fall further and further behind the rest. Finally, Meares and his dog team catch up.

Chancing on Weary Willy struggling with his sledge through a thick drift, the dogs sense easy prey. Like a hungry pack of wolves, the dogs lay into Willy, biting, tearing and mauling the poor creature as Meares and Gran swipe at them with ski poles. The vicious dogs have been travelling separately from the main party for a very good reason.

'Weary Willy will survive, but he'll never be the same and he won't be any use hauling,' says Scott. 'We'll have to go back and fetch the sledge. And I'm going to send three of the weakest ponies back.'

'All those ponies are good for is working into the ground,' grumbles Oates. 'Fit for dog food and not much besides. I think we should work them out completely, then shoot the worst of them and stash the meat for next summer.'

'We'll not be working any of them to death,' says Scott sternly. 'I can't have such a cruel waste of life.' Scott can't afford for any to die. He needs all the ponies for the journey to the pole.

'Not sure this is the right place for such noble ideas, sir. Those crocks won't get far. Before long, you'll not only be feeding them to the dogs, but eating them yourself.'

If Oates wasn't such a valuable member of the team and so devoted to caring for the ponies, Scott might order him back to Cape Evans. Personalities aside, Scott knows he'll need that sort of steely character when he pushes on towards the pole. They don't need to be friends, just allies.

Blood-splattered snow surrounds Weary Willy's sledge. Its runners are hidden deep under the crusty surface. Just as they free it from the drift, the sledge becomes stuck again, acting more like an anchor than a means of transport.

It takes forever for Scott, Wilson and Bowers to haul it the final distance over the wind-hardened waves of snow to their camp. It's a brief taste of what the ponies have endured for weeks on end.

The men are exhausted. The animals are exhausted. Despite their generous food allowance, the ponies and dogs are so hungry they eat their own excrement. The sky is bruised with dark cloud. Everything is grey and cold and bleak. The mental strain of walking without a fixed point in the distance to aim for is almost too much. Scott blows his whistle, calling a halt to their march. He gathers the men together and delivers his verdict:

'The terrible condition of the snow, the steady decline of the ponies and the worsening weather all point to a return to Cape Evans. I think it's time we headed home.'

Nobody objects. Almost 1000 kilograms of supplies are offloaded. One Ton Depot, they call it. A black flag fluttering atop a tall bamboo pole marks the final stop on their march. Several empty sledges are jammed upright into the snow to provide more height to the structure. It's visible for miles. But One Ton is 48 kilometres short of where they planned to stash their final supply depot. It's not a vast shortfall in distance, but the decision will cost at least three of the men their lives.

CHAPTER TWELVE

The dogs are weary. Hungry and thin, they've travelled 125 kilometres in three days. Pulling a sledge is work enough – there are no free rides for Scott, Wilson, Cherry-Garrard and Meares, who must jog alongside. Tiring as it is, the exercise keeps them warm. There's no heat from the sun when it is perched so low on the horizon. But visibility is good. Mt Terror rises to the north. Stencilled against the sky in black and white, it appears close enough to touch. In actual fact, it is more than 100 kilometres away.

'I believe if we cut diagonally across from here, we'll bypass Corner Camp and be closer to where we need to be,' says Scott. 'It's a shortcut of sorts. The weather looks settled enough to attempt it.'

The men are all in agreement. A shortcut makes sense. Besides, they don't need to wait for the others. The depot-laying party has split into three. There are clear tracks to follow home and they've agreed that each team will maintain its own pace and rendezvous at Safety Camp. The four men maintain a good pace. They've already covered several kilometres on a reasonably good surface when Cherry notices a drop in the level of the Barrier. It's a bad sign.

'Wilson!' he yells.

Wilson sees it too. Jumping onto the sledge, he manages to stop the dog team before they fall into the nasty crevasse. But just as he shouts a warning, Wilson sees Scott's team disappear two by two. It's as if the dogs were chasing a rabbit down a hole. Scott leaps onto the sledge, weighing it down as it starts to tip forward. All his dogs are gone, all except the leader Osman. Poor Osman grips to the snow, a crouching fearful wretch. His harness supports twelve other dogs, who are now dangling by their traces. The animals bark and yowl and scrape their paws on the blue ice walls, hoping to run back up to the surface.

The men work fast. The tent and sleeping bags are offloaded first – to lose them would be very serious. Next they safeguard the sledge, pegging it in place. Then to

Osman. They secure his end of the line then cut the dog free of the harness that is crushing him with such tremendous force. He scampers away across the snow, relieved, alive and totally unconcerned about his friends hanging in the void.

'Can everyone get a firm footing?' Scott asks. 'I don't want any of you disappearing in there with them.'

Nobody wants to be a hero. Each man is grateful to have escaped death.

Meares inches to the edge of the crevasse. 'Two have slipped their harnesses already. They're on a snow ledge about twenty metres down.'

'We'll worry about them later. Let's haul these ones up before we lose any others,' says Scott, removing his reindeer mitts to better grip the leather traces. He winces. Encouraging already numb fingers to take the strain in such biting cold is agony.

'One, two, three, pull!'

The dogs howl as their harnesses tighten around their skinny frames. The sound is amplified in the narrow space. Two dogs start to fight. Dangling within reach of each other, they snarl and bite and lash out, perhaps blaming each other for their predicament.

'Pull!' Scott's face turns crimson with effort.

Wilson squeezes his eyes shut. Cherry's glasses steam up. Meares swears as the frozen leather straps cut into his bare hands.

70

Two by two, the dogs appear over the ragged lip of the crevasse. Whimpering, they claw desperately at freedom as Cherry cuts them free of their harnesses. Judging by the way they hobble away from the hole, a few have sustained internal injuries.

'What of those two? The ones down there on the ledge,' Meares asks. 'How on earth are we going to reach them?'

'Somebody will have to go down,' says Scott.

Wilson shakes his head.

'Meares?' says Scott. 'They're your dogs. What do you say?'

'They may be my dogs but it's also my life,' says Meares, grim faced. 'I'm not going down there for a couple of bad-tempered brutes. They're as likely to attack me.'

'Then I shall have to go,' says Scott.

'Robert, it's madness,' says Wilson. 'They're only dogs. It's not worth the risk.'

'Look, they've curled up and fallen asleep,' says Cherry. 'Perhaps we should leave them.'

Scott is already roping up. 'I'll not leave those two down there to die slowly of hunger.'

'Please, Robert. Listen to me . . .' pleads Wilson.

'Lower me down. That's an order.'

Unable to disobey orders, the men lower Captain Scott down the crevasse. It's impossibly deep, a blue, bottomless chasm. Scott has fallen down a few in his time, but only to the length of a sledging harness – never to this depth. He looks around the crevasse with great interest. *So much to learn about their formation, their lifespan, the stresses acting on them*, he thinks. This is the sort of scientific work he's passionate about – exploring new frontiers, extending the limits of current thinking. He may not be scientifically trained himself, but it is a thrill to be involved in furthering the research of the expedition's own men of science, even in a superficial way.

The two dogs have made themselves quite comfortable while the frenzied rescue effort has been playing out above them. Unsure of the reception he'll get, Scott is relieved to meet with wagging tails, not snarling. Detaching himself from the alpine rope, he ties it around the first dog. One at a time, they are winched to safety.

Being this deep in the ice is surreal. Scott wishes he had a thermometer to find out the temperature of the Barrier itself. This far down, he's sure to get an accurate reading.

His thoughts are interrupted by noise on the surface. He can hear shouts, barking.

'Wait there!' Cherry calls down the hole.

'Well, I can hardly go elsewhere,' calls Scott, rather bemused by the delay. Whatever can be wrong? He peers along the snow ledge. Tests it with a few tentative steps.

72

It continues the length of the crevasse with its undulating aquamarine walls. With a bit more time he could take a look, see where it leads. This unexpected opportunity is simply too good.

Up on the surface, Wilson and Meares stand helpless. Cherry looks on, terrified. Fighting has broken out among all twenty-six dogs. Tearing at each other, howling in anguish, the dogs are a tangled mess of harnesses, teeth and torn flesh. To separate them is impossible. In the end, Meares grabs a tent pole and slices the air with it, whipping the troublemakers into submission. But not before a good deal of blood and fur is spread about the battlefield.

'Good grief, what happened here?' asks Scott, when he's finally dragged back up.

'Mutiny, I suspect,' says Wilson with a wry smile. 'It seems not all dogs appreciate being led over a precipice.'

The dogs are lucky to be alive. The ponies have suffered their own troubles on the long road home. Two have dropped dead of exhaustion. More death is to come.

CHAPTER THIRTEEN

Reunited at Safety Camp, the sledging teams reorganise. Wilson and Meares will continue with the dogs. Scott and Oates will stay back and help lead the ponies across the sea ice to Hut Point. Weary Willy is nearing the end and has to be helped to his feet. After feeding him a hot oat mash, Oates leads the ailing pony for as long as he can with Scott and Gran pulling his sledge on skis. Even without a load, the pony struggles. When Weary Willy collapses, they build a snow wall to shelter him from the wind and set up camp. Nobody expects he'll last the night out – he never fully regained his strength after standing three days in the open during the dreadful blizzard.

Meanwhile Bowers, Cherry and Crean battle on with four ponies and sledges. They've made good distance but remain unsure of conditions further on. It's later in the season and colder – the sea ice should have solidified by now. Casting out from the Barrier edge, they can see it is a good two and a half metres thick. They set up camp. They eat. They fall into a deep sleep.

'What was that?' Bowers wakes with a start. A loud snore issues from Cherry's sleeping bag. Bowers closes his eyes again. But there it is again – that sound. It's not a snore. It's coming from outside.

Bowers groans. 'If that pony has got into the oats again, I'll wring his bloody neck.' He crawls out of his sleeping bag and fiddles with the ties securing the tent flap. Sticking his head out, Bowers gasps.

'Cherry, Crean, we're floating out to sea.'

The two men are immediately on their feet, grabbing shoes, snow clothes. Bowers disappears outside, nothing but socks on his feet. He's already hauled two sledges from a neighbouring floe when the others appear from the tent.

'Crikey,' says Crean, staring at the open water that stretches out around them. 'You're right, Birdie. We're heading out to sea.'

'Where's Guts?' asks Cherry, bewildered.

Bowers says, 'He's gone. The ice split right underneath him.'

'What do we do?' Cherry feels panic rising in his chest. *Keep calm, keep calm*, he tells himself.

'We've been in a few tight places, but this is the limit,' says Bowers, under his breath.

The colour has drained from Cherry's face. Bowers regrets his comment immediately. If he's scared out of his wits, he must hide it from Cherry at all costs. He locks eyes with Crean. A seasoned navy man, he will play along with the brave act.

'So what's our plan?' asks Crean in a matter-of-fact tone.

'Luckily we're all on the one floe. We need to pack up camp and harness the ponies so we're ready to move at a moment's notice. The wind is from the east so we must move westward. Our only option is to move from floe to floe and try to get back onto the Barrier somehow.'

The tide is going out. Bowers understands that they're being carried towards open water. *Keep it together*, he thinks, clenching his teeth. *Keep it together*. Crean is acting like he's seen it all before, even though he hasn't. What he does know is that nothing lies between them and the Ross Sea.

Time and again, other floes pass by just out of reach. Frustration may lead to recklessness if the men's luck doesn't change. The uncertainty of it all drags on for an hour or more. Then by some sweet reversal, the current begins to work in their favour.

'It's coming closer,' breathes Bowers. 'Another few inches and we should be fine. Ready? Go.'

The men jump the ponies one by one to the next floe then haul the sledges over as quick as they can. The sledges are long enough to act as bridges when the distance between floes becomes too wide for the men to jump safely. After a few times, they've got the hang of it. Cherry even manages a smile and shares a chocolate bar from his pocket.

It's been several hours and they've managed to get closer to the Barrier edge. They stare at the ice cliffs – six metres high and impossible to climb. Besides, a nasty swell makes getting close to the Barrier edge simply too danger-ous – their floe wouldn't last the pounding it would get, and from time to time huge chunks of the ice cliffs collapse into the wash. To make matters worse, Bowers notices black fins rising from the water. Four, five, six orcas. They're hunting seals in the chopped-up sea ice. Bobbing up and down, the killers check out the floe and its unsteady cargo. A veritable feast on ice.

'One of us will have to go it alone,' says Bowers. 'Go and get the captain. He'll know what to do.'

'I'll go,' Crean says. 'I reckon I can get onto the Barrier a bit further on. See, over there.'

'Perhaps we could pitch the tent,' says Cherry. 'To mark our position better.'

'Excellent!' says Bowers, feeling like any plan is better than none.

Bowers mounts the theodolite and watches Crean through the telescope as he jumps from floe to floe like a frog skipping across lily pads. When he sees Crean clamber onto the Barrier, he breathes a sigh of relief. At least one of them has reached safety.

Cherry can't take his eyes off the killer whales. Neither can Bowers. It's going to be a long wait. Both men could have followed Crean's lead, but neither wants to leave the ponies and everything on the sledges to save themselves. It just doesn't seem right.

'You evil creatures,' Bowers says as a whale bobs straight up in the water and studies the two men with its beady black eye. 'You can forget about eating me for supper.'

The day drags. They move when they can and when they can't, they wait. In the late afternoon, they feed the ponies. For them, it's just another day in Antarctica.

With the shifting tide their floe drifts ever closer to the Barrier edge. Once they're close enough, Cherry and Bowers haul the sledges and supplies onto a higher floe that might prove to be a useful step up. Using an upturned sledge as a ladder, they could easily scramble onto the Barrier. But for the ponies. For them, a ladder is of little use.

They hear voices. Crean's head appears over the Barrier edge. Oates and Scott are with him.

'My dear chaps, I'm so glad to see you safe!' says Scott, beaming. 'Let's get you up here quick.'

'We can't just leave everything.' Bowers squints up at the captain.

'I don't care a thing about the ponies and sledges. I want to see you up here on the Barrier in one piece before I agree to anything else.' Scott extends an arm for Bowers to grab. Oates has Cherry by the jacket and is hauling him across to safety. The motion causes the floe to shift away. A dark ribbon of water opens up. The three ponies huddle together as they drift beyond reach.

Crean grimaces. Bowers can't believe it. After all their efforts to save them, there's nothing they can do except watch the ponies float away – to certain death.

'Poor beasts,' he says. 'If I could, I would rather kill them myself than picture them starving on that floe out on the Ross Sea, or eaten by those killers.'

It's late. The men decide to make camp. But Bowers can't rest. He insists on walking further along the coast, hoping to get close enough to save the three ponies. Nobody holds much hope of success but he returns several hours later with good news.

'They're back,' he cries. 'We can get to them, they're not far.'

Oates follows Bowers back to the spot. He's right. Using their ice axes, they drag the floe close enough to

79

lead one pony ashore. But the commotion has attracted some sinister onlookers. There are now more than a dozen orcas thrusting their snouts out of the water, spooking the ponies and making it impossible for the men to safely jump them across. Sensing their moment, the killer whales strike. There's a heavy splash, then another. Both ponies are in the water, their eyes stretched wide with panic.

Bowers runs out onto the floe, wanting to do something but realising he is totally helpless.

'Bowers!' shouts Oates. 'It's over.'

Oates jumps across. The ice platform wobbles under their weight. The ponies swim about the floe, their heads straining out of the water.

Oates tugs Bowers' arm. 'Come on, it's not safe here. We'll be next if we're not careful. There's nothing we can do for them.'

'We must do something.' Bowers looks pleadingly at Oates. 'I can't let them be torn apart by those ghastly beasts.'

Oates nods his agreement. He hates to do it but there is no alternative. The two men lift their ice axes high above their heads and bring them down with terrible speed. Death is instant, painless. The sea around the two ponies turns a bloody red.

CHAPTER FOURTEEN

Hot, plentiful meals, warm beds, dry clothes and the first bath anyone has had for close to three months – the early days of being back at Cape Evans are pure heaven. The depot-laying mission took a lot longer than planned; it's already the end of April. The sea ice that was to serve as their road home from Hut Point had been carried away. With no way forward and nobody crazy enough to attempt to cross the ice falls at the base of Mt Erebus, the party had to remain a tantalising 15 kilometres from home, eating seals and burning blubber to keep themselves warm at Hut Point for nearly a month.

Amid the cheer of the return, Scott remains silent. He has a lot on his mind. Not only has he lost six of the eight ponies he took on the depot-laying trip, he has since received some distressing news. A confidential letter from Lieutenant Campbell, who travelled aboard the *Terra Nova* further east along the Great Ice Barrier, has thoroughly soured his homecoming. He has kept the news to himself for too long. Sharing it with the men cannot be delayed any further. With a heavy heart, Captain Scott calls everyone together.

'I'm afraid I have some bad news. It appears that our worst fears have been realised.' Scott hesitates in front of the assembled men. Once he makes this announcement, nothing will be the same. 'Norwegian explorer Roald Amundsen intends to reach the pole before us. While I have known this to be the case for some time, I have recently received confirmation that he and his men are camped on the Great Ice Barrier to the east of us. I understand that his small team are well prepared for a push south in the early spring and at this stage are positioned some 110 kilometres closer to the pole than we are.'

Anger boils over. There's much shouting. That somebody would do such a thing – to steal the major objective of their expedition! It is ungentlemanly. It is without honour. It is beyond belief.

Scott raises his voice above the din. He hates the effect the news has had on the men. If only he could carry the knowledge of it himself, spare them the shock of it, he would. But the time has come. They deserve to know.

'As there is nothing we can do to ward off our competition, I suggest we stick to our original plans. We must block out all thoughts of what the Norwegian presence on the ice might imply for our own chances of success. We must go forward and do our best for the honour of our country. Without fear or panic.

'We are well prepared. Our team is composed of some of the finest men in the British Empire. Our ambitious program of scientific research will continue. I know that the knowledge we are acquiring will benefit generations of polar adventurers to come. I therefore encourage you to take to every task with the utmost dedication and pride. I am confident of a favourable outcome.'

The room erupts in loud applause.

Oates stands up. 'So, a race is it? Well, if that's what the rascal Amundsen wants, let's give him one!'

The men cheer.

'How do you come to know all this, Captain Scott?' calls Cherry when the noise dies down.

'I received a telegram back in October when I was in Melbourne. It was from Amundsen. He advised me of his intention to claim the pole for the Norwegian king. It appears that he has kept his plans secret for some time, not even sharing them with the crew of his ship.'

'The scoundrel!' shouts Bowers. 'Fancy lying to your men. Not letting on where they're going. It's shameful.'

'Apparently they all thought they were headed to the Arctic,' adds Scott. 'They didn't learn the truth until they were some way into their voyage.'

'I'm surprised it didn't end in mutiny,' Ponting says.

'And you know for a fact that they've arrived?' Oates asks. 'That they're actually here on the ice?'

'Yes,' Scott hesitates again. He clears his throat. The last thing he wants is for his voice to break and reveal how desperate he feels about the whole thing. 'Lieutenant Campbell and his party came across Amundsen's ship, the *Fram*, at anchor in the Bay of Whales. The *Terra Nova* was to leave Campbell and his five men to explore the area inland. As it happens, because Amundsen is camped where they hoped to stay themselves, they have headed northward to Cape Adare instead.'

The burly Welshman Taff calls out, 'Let's go there now and have it out with them. Over to the Bay of Whales with our fists and show Amundsen and all his fellows they're not welcome.'

There's much shouting in support of Taff's idea.

However, they all know a punch-up will not solve their problem. Like it or not, a race to the pole is inevitable.

'Today I am ashamed to be Norwegian,' says Gran loudly to the room.

Ponting gives him a pat on the back. 'Not to worry old chap. We all know whose side you're on.'

Oates nods and adds, 'And we all know whose side will win!'

CHAPTER FIFTEEN

Six ponies gone. It's a terrible blow. Only ten remain for the polar journey. And of those, several look unlikely to last out the winter. *Are they really such feeble specimens?* wonders Scott. *Is Oates right after all?*

Depot laying has been an education. Scott is still confident that these ponies can haul heavy loads. But struggling as they do on all but the hardest-packed snow, it's now quite clear that the Manchurian ponies have serious limitations. The snow conditions out on the Barrier were appalling – worse than the surface he encountered with Wilson and Shackleton in 1902. And the extreme cold also took its toll on the animals. In particular, the blizzard dealt a death blow to more than a couple of the weaker ones. For this reason alone, Scott cannot hope to set out for the pole until late spring. It's a delay he can ill afford with Amundsen breathing down his neck.

Lieutenant Campbell's letter was quite specific. Amundsen has more than two hundred dogs. No ponies at all. Scott must face facts. If the depot-laying trip is anything to go by, Amundsen has the advantage. Dogs might not have the strength of the ponies but they can pass over the softest snow without sinking. Their stamina keeps them going all day, with enough energy left for a spectacular dog fight should the opportunity arise. Thick fur coats keep them warm in even the most bitterly cold conditions. Blizzards are nothing but a chance to rest up.

Timing is everything. Scott cannot leave for the pole until summer conditions prevail. With his dogs, Amundsen can set out whenever the mood takes him. Amundsen knows his dogs will die of exhaustion. His plan is undoubtedly to feed the dead dogs to their surviving comrades. Amundsen will probably eat the dog meat himself. It's not something Scott would choose to do but he understands the advantage Amundsen will gain in not carrying as many provisions on his sledges.

Scott frowns. His reasons for coming to Antarctica are so many and so varied. For an ambitious man, the chance to be first at the South Pole is a strong motivator. So is his love of king and country and his sense of pride in bringing honour and glory to the British Empire. But there's more to it than that. He feels alive in this place, invigorated by the possibility of contributing to the body of human knowledge. Antarctica may appear as an icy wasteland but it is in fact a vast laboratory with limitless secrets to uncover. Determination is the key. One must be strong to uncover them.

So what are his strengths? What could possibly count in his favour? His men, for one. They were excellent men to begin with. But now they have fire in their bellies. Perhaps the Norwegian threat will be all the encouragement they need to claim victory for Britain. Besides, it seems doubtful that Amundsen's dogs have patriotism coursing through their veins.

His men can haul sledges over difficult terrain far better than dogs. All they need are good rations and the right mental attitude. Scott himself has manhauled 850 kilometres across the Great Ice Barrier during his *Discovery* expedition in 1902. While it is far from pleasant, it is entirely possible.

Of course there is another possibility that could help them against the Norwegians. What if some tragedy should befall Amundsen? What if he and his men all perished?

Scott shakes his head. The thought is too awful, too real. The truth is, perishing on the way to the pole is a very real possibility for all of them.

CHAPTER SIXTEEN

'Do you not have anything else?' somebody calls out.

'Something with a bit less flavour?' shouts another.

'Something you don't have to chew for two hours?'

Once again, the dinnertime conversation focuses on Clissold's latest culinary offering. Roast penguin breast.

'Is it more bird, or more fish?' asks Ponting, examining the flesh on the end of his fork.

'Chicken it is not,' grunts Oates, ramming a slice into his mouth and clamping it shut, lest his taste buds reject the meat outright. 'But it won't kill you. Best get it down quick.'

'I've heard the trick with cooking penguin is to separate the meat from the blubber as soon as possible. The blubber's where the foul fishy odour comes from.' Wilson has done his fair share of penguin butchering. In the interests of science, of course. Although Clissold is always happy to take any scraps and turn them into strange new delights.

'I do prefer seal,' says Cherry-Garrard. 'Meat to eat. Fuel for your fire. Oil for your lamp. Leather for your shoes. An antidote to scurvy.'

'Speaking of scurvy, it's medicine time.' Taff pours each man a small glass of lime juice. The men wince as they suck it down. They'd far rather have a glass of port or sherry to chase down the evil-tasting penguin.

'We are to start a newspaper,' Scott announces after dinner. 'It's a bit of a tradition since *Discovery* days, isn't it Wilson? *The South Polar Times* will once again entertain and inform all those wintering over in Antarctica.'

Wilson winks at Scott. He hopes the paper will be as successful as it was last time in keeping the men's spirits up over the dark months. Forced to spend many a long hour inside the Cape Evans hut, the men must have something to keep their minds occupied, some good cheer, some way to relieve the tension of close confinement.

'I have asked Cherry to be its editor,' continues Scott. 'I know each of you has his own particular talents. I encourage you all to submit material for publication – whatever you like. Illustrations, scientific articles, stories, poems – all of it will remain anonymous. I know Cherry will accept it grate-fully and type it up for distribution.'

'I already have some illustrations for you,' says Wilson, proudly holding up a drawing of Birdie Bowers that makes him look half man, half penguin. The men hoot with laughter.

'Let's hope we don't have to eat that one for dinner!' somebody shouts.

Bowers sticks his tongue out at Wilson but he's having fun too, already planning his comic revenge on the good doctor.

'And as winter confines us to our hut, I would also like to organise a series of evening lectures. We have an extraordi-nary diversity of talent and training in our people; it would be difficult to imagine a group of people with so many differ-ent experiences – physicists, geographers, sailors, soldiers, artists, biologists, men of medicine and meteorologists. I look forward to hearing all your stories and seeing out winter a more knowledgeable individual than I am today.'

It's a frightening prospect for some. For others, it's an opportunity to get up in front of a room full of men and jaw on endlessly about their particular field of interest. Some lectures will be informative. Some lectures will be enter-taining. Some lectures will be so boring that the men will struggle to stay awake. But at least they will have some form of occupation during their long evenings.

CHAPTER SEVENTEEN

The sun is now a slave to the horizon. Never straying, it sinks lower day by day. A strange twilight remains. Not morning, not evening, but something in between. Scientific work becomes a priority. Dr Simpson, the meteorologist, is running experiments, sending instruments up to measure air temperature using large silk balloons filled with hydrogen. Bowers is in the thick of it, helping where he can to get the instruments airborne then setting out across the sea ice to find them when they fall back down to earth. Meanwhile, the geologists are busy identifying and cataloguing the rock samples they collected in the Western Mountains while the others were laying the depots.

Knowing that they will soon lose the benefits of natural light, the artists are also hard at work. Dr Wilson spends his days sketching the landscape. He's found a sheltered spot up the hill some distance and works in frenzied bursts, replacing his gloves every few minutes to restore some warmth to his frozen fingers. Low light has transformed Cape Evans. Wilson's palette, long dominated by white, black and blue, is suddenly alive with pink, violet and red.

Capturing the change in seasons occupies Herbert Ponting's days too. He dreads the approach of winter, when darkness will prevent him from taking any photographs outside. He can't imagine the inside of the Cape Evans hut will provide much in the way of natural beauty. The dark room he has organised for himself will be his refuge. But for now he still has the wonders of nature to fill his camera lens. Setting out with a sledge piled high, Captain Scott is a willing assistant, happy to lug equipment far and wide and keen to learn as much as he can from the photographer. Ponting has his movie camera. The seals are his stars, squeezing out from cracks in the ice to flop around on cue. How ungainly they are. And how trusting!

Oates, Crean, Evans and Cherry-Garrard exercise the ponies. So does Clissold – it's nice for the cook to have an opportunity to get out of the kitchen and spend time with animals he has no intention of turning into a stew. He runs to and fro, filling his lungs with sweet, fresh air until his teeth buzz with the cold. Before long he'll be back at his coal range preparing supper. Pleased to be out from the confines of their stalls, the ponies are keen to get away from their handlers. With the ponies running off into the thick mist that often surrounds Cape Evans, this joy can fast turn into a terrible chore.

More exercise is to be had on the makeshift football pitch. It's a great opportunity to get hearts pumping and spirits up ahead of a period of limited physical activity. Atkinson is by far the best player now that his heel has recovered. He dodges, tackles and scores many a winning goal. When he's not kicking footballs, Atkinson checks the fish traps he's set in deep holes cut into the sea ice. While the men enjoy eating the fish he catches, Atkinson is more interested in research. He bends over his microscope for hours at a time, examining the parasites that burrow deep in the flesh and guts of his Antarctic fish. He's already discovered many new species.

Every day the light retreats a little bit more. Despite the gloom, there is an air of contentment, a sense of shared purpose at Cape Evans. Everybody helps out with the little jobs that need doing inside and out. There are plenty of repairs and many improvements to make to their equipment. Nobody wants to appear lazy or unwilling. They all know Scott won't want the lazy and unwilling to join him at the pole.

Even the men on the night watch do their part, making scientific observations while everybody else sleeps. On the evenings when clear skies allow uninterrupted views of the Aurora Australis, whoever is on duty is expected to watch the spectacular trails of light, jotting down notes on the dominant hues of the aurora displays, their intensity and range of movement. It's a little spooky being outside in the dark and watching the colours ripple and uncoil like a majestic sky snake. No amount of telling themselves that they're contributing to Dr Simpson's work on the earth's magnetic field seems to make a difference – the spectacle feels more supernatural than scientific.

Wilson welcomes winter. His most exciting zoological work can only be undertaken during the dark months. Emperor penguin eggs are what he's after. He believes that if he can get his hands on some and study the development of their feathers, he might discover an evolutionary link between birds and reptiles. It's not going to be easy. The emperor penguins only lay their eggs in the depths of winter. In the middle of nowhere. Cape Crozier is known for its severe weather. Blizzards there often last more than a week. Wilson will need to travel in complete darkness. But he won't be going alone.

'Cherry, may I come in?' Wilson pops his head over the stone wall that Cherry-Garrard has been working on for three days.

'What do you think?' smiles Cherry, sitting back and admiring his handiwork.

'I think it is quite the best igloo you have constructed yet.' Wilson gives the stone wall a knock with the side of his fist. 'Very robust. Should withstand the winds at Cape Crozier no problem. And the roof?'

'Canvas for the roof and door. We'll want a bit of ventilation with the blubber stove going.'

'Yes,' says Wilson, wrinkling his nose. 'Bit smelly, that greasy black smoke.'

'I've been testing it with seal blubber. I'm assuming penguin blubber burns just as well.'

'Burns like a dream, Cherry. And it will be plentiful. You'll see, there are thousands of birds at the nesting grounds. It will save us lugging fuel all that way under our own steam.'

Birdie Bowers has volunteered to join Cherry and Wilson. He's desperate to strike out and do something other than assorted chores around the hut. He may be small, but Bowers is considered to be one of the ablest manhaulers on the expedition. He's also the one who can withstand the cold. Wilson and Cherry will need his pulling power. The winter conditions are too severe for animals. Even if the ponies or dogs could withstand the freezing winter temperatures, Scott would be most reluctant to see any of the animals head off midwinter. With only ten of his original nineteen ponies remaining, Scott cannot risk losing any others or falling short with the dog teams. As important as penguin eggs are to Wilson's research, they cannot take resources away from the expedition's main objective – reaching the pole.

CHAPTER EIGHTEEN

Oates rolls his eyes at Taff and mouths, 'When will it end?'

Taff sighs loudly and shifts in his seat. He's enjoyed the evening lectures – learning about ice formation from Wright, rainbows and auroras from Simpson, geography from Griffith Taylor. Ponting's exotic slide show about Burma had him wide-eyed with interest. But Debenham's talk has been pure torture. For more than an hour he has droned on about volcanoes. Even Scott, who is so eager to take notes and always asks a thousand questions, has fallen asleep in his chair. How could a topic so explosive and dramatic be explained in such deadly dull terms? Debenham concludes his lecture. The room clears in a flash. Nobody wants to be left alone with the scientist – they're all terrified of getting homework.

There's far more enthusiasm for the High Festival of Midwinter. Roast beef, Yorkshire puddings, fried potatoes, Brussels sprouts and plum pudding. It may be the middle of June in Antarctica but the feast laid out on the table looks more like a Christmas dinner in England.

The Festival of Midwinter is Captain Scott's idea, a symbolic celebration to mark the mid-point in the polar calendar. Champagne is flowing. Everyone wants to raise a toast. To their leader. To their expedition. To their success. Union Jacks hang from the rafters. The hut is festooned with colourful sledging flags. The table is decorated with candles, bowls of chocolates and dried fruit. The men are in high spirits, dancing, singing, playing the piano, telling jokes and arguing about politics. Bowers appears at the end of the evening with a Christmas tree that he has made from a stick, some string and thousands of strips of green craft paper – goodness knows where he hid it.

'I have a surprise for you!' Wilson calls out, lifting up a bulging sack. 'My dear sister insisted I bring these presents south to give you all some joy in the middle of winter.' He makes his way around the room, handing out little packages.

'A pop gun!' cries Oates. 'Just what I need to get those ponies moving.'

'I've got a sponge,' says Crean. 'What do I need with a sponge?'

'I'll have it!' says Oates, grabbing the misshapen yellow blob.

'You can have my whistle too, Titus,' says Lieutenant Evans, tossing it high over Ponting's head.

Anton the Russian does a wild Cossack dance. A few others try to copy him but fall flat on their backsides. They laugh so much they cannot get back to their feet. The champagne is having an effect on the mood of the evening. Very little work will be done tomorrow.

'Are you sweating, Cherry?' asks Oates.

Cherry runs his hand over his forehead. 'No.'

Oates blows his whistle. 'Yes you are!' He wipes Cherry's face with the sponge, which has soaked up some mystery liquid from the table.

Cherry removes his glasses and dries them on his shirt. 'You're in fine form, Oates.'

'If you want to please me very much you will fall down when I shoot you,' he says, popping his gun at Cherry. There's only one person who doesn't fall foul of Oates' pop gun during the night's celebrations. He's quite drunk, but even in his current state, Oates knows it wouldn't be a good idea to shoot the leader – not even in jest.

All the merrymaking in the hut has caused the dogs to start howling. Meares goes out to check on the animals but is soon back at the door.

'You need to see this!' he shouts.

Jackets, fur mitts and balaclavas are hastily pulled on. The crowd of revellers spills out onto the snow. The sight is incredible. The sky, from horizon to horizon, is alive with the aurora – the most vivid display anyone has ever witnessed. The lights ripple like curtains of colourful ribbon in a heavenly breeze. Nobody speaks. They watch the luminous show over their heads, awed by its strangeness and dwarfed by its immense scale. It's hard not to look for meaning. Something so beautiful is sure to be a good omen.

CHAPTER NINETEEN

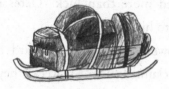

Two sledges, towed one behind the other. More than 340 kilograms of gear. Three men to pull. The penguin party has packed only essentials. But six weeks' provisions, scientific equipment for pickling and preserving, sleeping bags, ice axes, alpine rope and cooking oil adds up to a tremendous weight. Cherry-Garrard wriggles into his harness and adjusts his frost-etched spectacles. Perhaps Lashly would have been a more robust choice than himself.

'This winter travel is a new and bold venture,' says Scott to Ponting, who has had to use a powerful flash to capture the departing men.

'Those three men are certainly bold,' agrees Ponting. 'I'm not sure I'd be prepared to head out in the blackest night in search of penguin eggs. I've only spent half an hour outside and I cannot wait to wrap my hands around a mug of hot tea.'

'Well, they're the right men for the job – that is certain,' Scott says. 'May good luck go with them.'

'They'll need more than luck.' Oates says, stamping warmth back into his feet.

Wilson, Bowers and Cherry-Garrard disappear. The polar night has claimed them. Six weeks they'll be gone. No man has ever attempted a midwinter journey in Antarctica, let alone one so ambitious. The Cape Crozier rookery is the only one of its kind, and very remote. Wilson has been there before, during the *Discovery* expedition in 1902. It was spring, and he saw chicks. From that, he assumes that the penguins must incubate their eggs during winter. It's an educated guess. But he does not know for sure. Wilson hopes the whole unpleasant journey won't be for nothing.

For the moment the pulling is comfortable. The sea ice towards Hut Point is firm and smooth, and the sledge slides easily for the first few hours. Stopping for lunch is their first trial. Winter closes around them like a slowly tightening fist. The wind has picked up and they must hurry to erect the flapping tent and free up their cooker and provisions for the very first meal. It's a tricky business, not least because it's dark. And any task becomes more difficult when wearing bulky reindeer mitts – but they dare not remove them in such bitterly cold conditions. The thermometer reads 48 degrees below zero.

'These matches don't work,' complains Bowers, frantically trying to light their little primus stove. 'Pass me another box, Cherry.'

Cherry-Garrard fumbles in his pockets. 'Try this one.'

'Was it next to your body?' asks Bowers, striking again and again. 'Because these matches are all completely wet.'

Cherry holds a match up. It turns white – the moisture transforming into frost before his eyes. 'Hang on, I've got another.'

Same again. But this time it's their breath that freezes to the matches, rendering them useless.

Thankfully, the fourth box is dry. Nobody breathes until the primus is lit. A hot meal is all they have been dreaming about. But their break in the tent will be short-lived. They still have quite a distance to cover in the afternoon.

Mile after mile they lurch with their load. Talk is wasted effort. Breath freezes their balaclavas to their heads. Cherry's glasses are so frozen over that he cannot see a thing. But they're all travelling blind. The dark is all-encompassing. They're familiar with the route – to Hut Point at least. Once they get onto the Barrier and head east, the way forward will be completely new, a walk of faith into a black void.

Getting up onto the Ice Barrier proves more of a challenge than it was during depot laying. It would be impossible with the animals. The alpine rope comes in handy when they scale the low cliffs, then drag the sledges and supplies up and over. Thick mitts make the task fiendishly difficult. Try as he might, Cherry can't seem to get a decent grip on the rope, so he takes them off. The cold instantly attacks his exposed skin with an unexpected, savage intensity. Ten frostbitten fingers are the price he must pay.

'How could I have been so stupid?' he says that night in the tent. He turns his hands this way, then that, horrified at the enormous blisters that stretch his skin taut. The blisters rub horribly within his mitts. To make matters worse, the penetrating cold has turned the fluid in them to ice.

'You must wait until the ice in the blisters thaws, then you can prick them and relieve the pressure,' advises Wilson. 'Be prepared, it will be painful. But the relief you'll feel later will make it all worthwhile.'

Cherry-Garrard is scared. He feels out of his depth. Bowers and Wilson seem so confident, so capable, and here he is, frostbitten and stumbling on blindly a mere three days into the journey. He wants to cry with the pain. Should he be continuing with his hands in such a mess? The cold is inescapable. Even the sleeping bags can't protect them from its aggressive needling. The only time they are not suffering from it is when they are on the move – sweating profusely as they struggle with their load through the deep winter snow.

'Do we head back?' asks Wilson of his two travelling companions.

'No,' says Cherry.

'No,' says Bowers.

CHAPTER TWENTY

'Come on, you daft creature, there's nothing to be frightened of. It's only the wind.' Oates yanks on the tarpaulin to stop it flapping wildly in the wind and leads the pony back into its makeshift stable. White clouds of pony breath rise to the rafters, where it collects and freezes instantly.

'Ponies exercised. Dogs fed,' says Oates to Meares. 'I'm heading in. Time for my dinner.'

The hut is iced up. The entrance is a tunnel cut into the hardened snow drift that has the benefit of insulating much of the building from the prevailing winds. Atkinson appears at the door, followed by Gran. Fully clothed, they're obviously on their way out.

'It's closing in again, chaps,' Meares says. 'Not sure you'll want to be out.'

'Simpson's readings,' says Atkinson cheerily. 'Gran and I are going to nip out to check the north and south bay thermometers.'

'Didn't you and Taylor just do that?' Oates asks.

'No, not all three. We just checked the one on the hill. We need to check the two stations on the floe.'

Oates frowns. 'That wind's really picking up. It's easily minus 25 out there.'

'It's only a mile. We'll get there and back before dinner,' Atkinson gestures for Gran to hurry past Oates and Meares. 'I have a poor Norwegian ski instructor who has been cooped up in the hut all day. He's desperate for fresh air. Aren't you, Gran?'

Meares shrugs his shoulders and disappears into the warmth of the hut. Oates looks down at Atkinson's leather shoes and considers telling the surgeon to at least get some proper footwear on. But he doesn't.

Atkinson smiles. 'Truly, we'll be there and back before you know it.'

Winter at Cape Evans is all about waiting. The sun won't return for four months. The men read, play cards or chess, and write in their journals to pass the days. There are also plenty of adjustments to make to clothing, tents and equipment ahead of summer. When the weather allows, they run with the dogs and exercise the ponies, but now that the temperature has plummeted, nobody can stay out for long. The winds howl down to the coast from the frigid interior of the continent, sweeping away anything not tied down, and anyone not wearing crampons. The windswept snow polishes rusty dog chains, frays ropes and etches wood.

With dinner over, the men settle into their bunks for the evening. Even though the windows are covered with winter shutters, the wind has set the panes of glass rattling.

'Still no sign of Atkinson?' Oates asks, hoisting himself to his feet. He looks over at Gran who returned half an hour ago. 'It sounds like the beginnings of a blizzard.'

Meares puts down the pair of socks he's darning. 'Perhaps we should tell the captain.'

'We most definitely should.'

Scott is the only man with his own private room. It's not luxurious. A narrow bed, a shelf of books, a small desk with a few photos of his wife and young son attached to the wall, which he likes to rest his eyes on before sleep.

Oates gives a knock.

Scott looks up from his diary. 'Titus. What can I do for you?'

'It's Atkinson. He went to get a reading from Simpson's thermometer station and he's not back yet. He's wearing light clothing and leather boots.'

'How long has he been gone?' Scott screws on the lid of his fountain pen and closes his diary. The muscles of his jaw tighten as he reads the expression on Oates's face.

Gran joins Oates. 'We left about five-thirty,' the Norwegian says softly. 'It's now seven-fifteen.'

'Shall we go and look for him?' asks Oates.

A number of men are sent out short distances to shine lanterns around the hut and shout into the darkness. The moon appears from behind clouds, and with the increased visibility it is hoped that Atkinson will soon appear. But after another two hours, there is still no sign of him. The wind picks up again. Scott organises search parties with sledges, sleeping bags and brandy to help warm the lost man should he be found alive. Scott and Clissold remain at the hut, nervously waiting.

'Good news!' Meares calls through the door at midnight. 'We've got him, sir!'

Atkinson has been stumbling around in the darkness for more than six hours. Suffering from hypothermia, he babbles on in a confused way, trying to explain how he got so lost. One of his hands is badly frostbitten and covered by enormous blisters. His fingers look like bloated sausages.

'We have been extremely lucky,' says Scott when the search parties return. 'We must have no more of these unnecessary escapades. Let me remind you all that no scientific task is worth losing your life. And it is certainly not worth endangering the lives of others who must venture out and look for the lost.'

Ponting sidles up to Atkinson. 'I say, old chap. Once you've rested up a bit, might I take some photographs of that hand of yours? It is quite spectacularly awful.'

CHAPTER TWENTY-ONE

'I know I ask this rather a lot, Uncle Bill, but how much further?' Cherry's teeth chatter as he speaks. Only when he drops off into a shallow sleep does it stop.

Dr Wilson's head appears out of his sleeping bag. 'Only another 30 kilometres or so – not far now.' He's been using his breath to melt the ice that has invaded every layer of his clothing. But once the ice thaws, his clothes will be sodden – it's not a good start to the day, but there's nothing he can do to improve his situation. His hands, wet in their wool mittens, are white and wrinkled as if he's been in a bath too long.

The men have been trudging on for more than ten days, pushing further east, checking that Mt Erebus remains to their left and Mt Terror straight ahead whenever the moon chooses to shine on their woeful progress. When the moon hides, they feel the way with their feet, listening carefully for the hollow sound of crevasses.

'The worst thing for me,' says Bowers, keen to give voice to his frustration, 'is having to haul those sledges one at a time. Doubling back to get the second one, then heading back the way we've just come is torture. We travel three miles to get one mile closer to Cape Crozier.'

Relaying the sledges is a risky business. Blizzards can spring up quickly and cover the holes left by their feet in half an hour. But hauling two heavily laden sledges through deep snow in temperatures so cold the sledge runners don't glide but stick is impossible. For now there is no wind. It's a welcome relief after experiencing a cruel headwind for several days. The men can walk with candles to shine a path, an odd procession. Even without the wind, their clothing freezes rigid within seconds of leaving the tent. Only this morning, Cherry's clothes froze stiff to him as he turned to look into the distance. The rest of the day he was forced to march with his head looking back over one shoulder. At one point Bowers's camel-hair helmet is so frozen up that his head is encased in a solid block of ice.

It takes two men an hour to bash the third man out of his sledging gear at the end of each day, pummelling him with their fists to break the ice so they can then remove his harness and over-garments. It takes another hour for each of them to force open their frozen sleeping bags so they can thrust their aching bodies into the icy depths.

'The worst thing for me is the seven hours we must be in our sleeping bags,' says Cherry. His body shivers so violently in the sleeping bag that he's worried his back will break. 'I'm not sure men were designed for minus 50.'

'And what of our delicious meals?' interrupts Wilson. 'Don't they make this whole venture worthwhile?'

The men laugh. Pemmican – it's nobody's idea of a delicious meal. Regardless, they all fall on their rations at the beginning and end of each day as if it were a feast. But as good as the pemmican hoosh tastes to a frozen man, it is Dr Wilson's warmth, good nature and enthusiasm for their task that is keeping the men going.

'Do we head back?' asks Wilson.

'No,' says Cherry.

'No,' says Bowers.

CHAPTER TWENTY-TWO

Clissold dishes up his latest creation. Seal soup, followed by seal-liver curry and a stodgy pudding, which the men wolf down with steaming cups of sweet tea. With little else to keep the men busy, Clissold's meals have become the highlight of the winter days.

Knowing from his *Discovery* expedition how quickly men can succumb to scurvy, Scott keeps a close eye on everyone. Any sign of muscle aches, sore gums and skin bruising and he'll need to act quickly. As well as the compulsory lime juice dispensed to each man at the end of dinner, fresh meat seems to keep the potentially fatal illness at bay. And thanks to Clissold, there has been plenty of that. For now, constipation seems to be the most common complaint.

Tonight it is Scott's turn to deliver the evening lecture. Everyone listens intently as he outlines his plans for the expedition. While nearly everyone will set out together from Cape Evans on the early stages of the journey, nobody knows who will be chosen for the ultimate trek to the pole. They're all extremely eager to know. But that information is not part of this evening's talk. Instead, Scott sticks to the basics, such as the best route to take and the rations they'll need. 'I ask that everyone give thought to the problem, to freely discuss it and bring suggestions to my notice. If you think of any improvements to be made, you owe it to the expedition to share them. Remember we are in this together.'

Outside there is a blizzard. *We are in this together* – the phrase swirls around Scott's head as he tries to fall to sleep, as gusts batter the Cape beyond his window. *It's not true. We are not in this together.* More often than not, Scott feels completely alone, cast adrift in this adventure, with everyone looking to him for answers. Failure stalks him. He tries not to think of how much better Amundsen's chances are – but doubts flood his every waking minute. *Sleep*, Scott tells himself. Everything will feel better in the morning. His eyes come to rest on the photos of his wife and son.

This long absence; it must count for something. He'll make damn sure it does.

Out in the pony stalls, Oates adjusts the blubber stove to ensure it will see out the blustery night. Footsteps crunch behind him. Night watch. It's Taff. He strikes a match and lights his pipe.

'What do you think are our chances?' says Oates. 'Of being chosen?' He stands up straight but is still dwarfed by Taff's enormous bulk.

Taff shrugs and sends a heavy cloud of tobacco smoke from his mouth.

'Come on, Taff. You know him well enough. You pulled with him during *Discovery*, right?'

'That I did,' says Taff slowly. 'He's a tireless devil, is old Captain Scott. Pushes himself far beyond any navy man I know. And that's saying something.'

Oates sighs. 'I've changed my mind about Scott. That business with the snow shoes. And seeing him building the snow wall to protect his pony from the wind out on the Barrier. I must admit, I thought he was absolutely crackers. But before long, we were all doing the same, weren't we?'

'He knows his stuff.' Taff nods.

'So what do you think about our chances?' Oates asks again.

'Well, he won't be taking any of the scientific men. Except Wilson of course. He'll definitely take Wilson. If I

118

know Scott, he will want seamen – men that won't complain when they're cold, when they're hungry, when their feet go blue and they start pissing ice cubes,' Taff roars with laughter. 'And he'll want you, Titus. You might complain, but you're like him – you never give up.'

CHAPTER TWENTY-THREE

'I do not think anyone on earth has a worse time than an emperor penguin,' says Cherry-Garrard, who has made a special effort to wipe his spectacles so he can see Cape Crozier in the moonlight. He shouldn't have bothered. The empty panorama makes him feel even colder. He mashes his hands deeper into his mitts and grimaces.

'It's a desolate sight,' agrees Bowers.

From their vantage point 250 metres up Mt Terror, the men peer down at the bleak immensity and wonder how they will ever get down there. Pressure ridges of ice spread out below like a field ploughed by giants. Beyond is the Ross

Sea. Somewhere out there on the sea ice is the rookery and the precious penguin eggs they've risked their lives for.

For now, the men's priority is shelter – and getting the little stove stocked up with penguin blubber. Above all, they crave warmth and a chance to dry out. The march from Cape Evans has taken nineteen days, much longer than they expected. Everything is iced up. Chilled to the core, they've burned a lot more oil than they anticipated just trying to keep warm. The blubber stove is going to be vital for their survival at the Cape. What oil remains is needed for the journey home.

They choose a camp site with plenty of rocks to build their igloo, where a low ridge will hopefully provide some break from the wind. They won't be able to pack snow around the structure as they intended. It's packed extremely hard. Not even Wilson's ice axe can break chunks off. For now, they'll have to put up with the wind whistling through the gaps between the rocks. At least they can manage a roof – the canvas sheet tucked tightly under rocks with a sledge serving as a central rafter to stop the fabric drooping down. The tent, they will use to store equipment and provisions. It may be sturdy, but their shelter is way too small for anything other than their three sleeping bags and the blubber stove.

Getting to the penguins is indeed a puzzle. Even though Wilson has been to Cape Crozier before, everything has changed. It was springtime when he was here last, when the rocky landscape was mostly free of ice and snow.

The next day they pull themselves up ridges, slide down slopes and blunder into crevasses, all in near darkness, trying to find a way down to the rookery. They can hear the penguins. They can smell the rank odour of the nesting birds. But they can't see them. It's another dead end. The cold is sapping, mind-numbing. None of them has the appetite for more exploring. Retracing their steps, they battle back to the sparse comfort of their rocky shelter.

A second day. Again the men set off in search of penguins. Above their heads, stars fill the sky like static. Who knows what time of the day or night this is – they've long since given up keeping track. The ice cliff below their camp looks promising. They cut steps into the mountain-side to ease the way down. The lower they get, the less likely their route appears to offer success. But for a deep black hole disappearing into the wall of a pressure ridge, they would be stuck. Bowers shows courage. Carefully, he slithers through, wriggling worm-like until he can make out the other side. Beyond, it's flat. It's the rookery.

'Where are they all?' asks Bowers when Wilson and Cherry join him.

There are barely one hundred birds. The creatures bustle away, trumpeting a warning as the three egg snatch-ers look on, disappointed at such slim pickings.

'Let's be quick,' says Wilson, trying to appear bright. 'I fear bad weather will be upon us again soon.'

The penguins are easy prey. Balancing their eggs on their feet, they cannot move fast enough to escape capture. It's not an entirely fair fight.

'How many have you got there, Bowers?' calls Wilson in the gloom.

'Three penguins, six eggs,' Bowers calls back. 'Cherry?'

'I've got this fellow here. He's struggling a fair bit.' Cherry loses his grip on the massive penguin. It shoots away. Cherry starts to run after it but the penguin slides with such speed on its belly across the ice that there is no way a two-legged man can capture it.

'It's your lucky day, my friend,' he calls, picking up the egg the penguin left behind. Then he laughs. It's not an egg at all. It's an egg-shaped block of ice that the penguin has been nursing along, so desperate was he to sit on something.

Bowers is quickly skinning the penguins he's caught, stacking the blubber to one side.

'I can't understand it,' Wilson says, looking about. 'Perhaps we're too early. Or too late. There should have been thousands of birds here.'

'Not to worry. We've sorted ourselves out for fuel. And we've managed to lay our hands on some eggs. And that's

123

what we've struggled to this dreadful place for,' says Bowers, wiping his knife on the snow.

Cherry's thoughts are already on the blubber stove. Their warm shelter. The hoosh. But it's a long way back up the hill. 'How are we going to carry all this up to the camp, Uncle Bill?'

'Birdie will carry the blubber and we'll each put an egg in our mitts,' Wilson hands Cherry a couple of eggs. 'We'll manage. I promise a hot meal to every man who makes it home.'

'Well, I'm frozen and I'm hungry,' says Cherry. 'If there's a meal to be had, I'll get my eggs back up to camp in double-quick time.'

Bowers carefully slips his two eggs into his mittens before easing his hands in too. The egg is no longer warm but it's not yet frozen. 'Let's hope scrambled eggs are not on the menu.'

CHAPTER TWENTY-FOUR

The ridge behind their rocky igloo provides little relief from the wind. If anything, the polar blast hits the ridge at an angle and swirls with more intensity over their little camp.

'Things must improve,' sighs Wilson, nursing his bloodshot eye. The blob of boiling oil that spurted at him out of the blubber stove has put Cherry-Garrard off using the contraption.

'I'm so sorry, Bill. Perilous thing. I'm sure it's going to burst into flames,' he says, eyeing the stove with suspicion. Rolled tight in his sleeping bag, he's even colder now than he was at the rookery. He dreams of having something sweet in his mouth – a chocolate, a spoonful of jam, a sticky bun.

Bowers slurps his tea. 'There's little point using it with so much snow and wind whipping about in here anyway. Our home has so many holes it's more sieve than shelter.'

A fearful howl tears through the air. Another blizzard. It sucks at the canvas roof. The fabric makes a booming sound as it whips up and down. Each time the canvas is sucked up, the vacuum effect pulls more cold air and snow through cracks in the rocky walls. Every available piece of clothing is stuffed into the crevices. But the blizzard is building in intensity. Already they must shout to make themselves heard. Sleep is impossible. Dozing is the best the exhausted men can hope for. Cherry slips away, briefly dreaming himself back to Cape Evans to where the midwinter festival is still in full swing. He's just about to slip a spoonful of plum pudding into his mouth when Bowers screams in his ear.

'The tent!'

Cherry's foggy sleep-deprived mind tries to process the information. 'We're not in the tent,' he says wearily.

'Our tent has blown away!' Bowers yells again.

Wilson is also struggling to take it all in. 'Our tent?'

'The wind's taken it. Our things are strewn around outside – we need to gather everything up!'

Wilson seems suddenly more alert. The horror of it finally sinking in. Above him the canvas whips up and down. He cradles his eye. The pain is excruciating. He's not sure he can help.

'Cherry, help me, quick!' Bowers dashes outside. Within seconds various items begin to fly through the opening – spare boots, cans of cooking oil, a sack of provisions. 'I can't find the bottom of the cooker,' he shouts when Cherry joins him outside in the gale.

'But where's the tent?' Cherry screams into the wind. 'Where's our tent?'

Bowers doesn't answer. He hurls himself back into the shelter and makes for his sleeping bag.

Cherry follows, still utterly confused. 'But the tent. We can't get back home without a tent!'

'Cherry, get into your bag,' shouts Wilson.

A savage roar fills their ears. The canvas zigzags high into the sky like a demented butterfly and disappears. Their roof is gone. With nothing but the full fury of the blizzard above their heads, the three men burrow deep into their sleeping bags. Snow swirls about them. Soon it will cover them entirely. Completely alone in his thoughts, each man comes to the same conclusion. This is the end.

CHAPTER TWENTY-FIVE

The Cape Evans hut wakes to the smell of frying fish. Sunday – calm, comfortable, a day of reflection and relaxation. He's not a religious man but convention dictates that Captain Scott lead the church service. After an hour of rousing hymns and prayer, everyone heads out of the hut to stretch their legs in the dim light. The sky is uncluttered. Spring is but a glimmer, a promise just beyond reach. Some men choose skis, some strike out on foot, but everybody enjoys the fresh air and stillness. It really is a joy to be alive on such a splendid morning.

Lieutenant Evans and Tom Crean catch a crabeater seal. Atkinson checks for fish in his trap. He finds forty-three – it's a new record. It's good news for the men who are none too keen on seal meat.

In the crisp half-light, the mountains appear much closer than they actually are. The conditions draw Ponting out onto the bay with his cameras. The icebergs thrusting out of the ice near Inaccessible Island are too beautiful to ignore. From the hut, his flashes of magnesium look like lightning, illuminating the sky and bouncing off everything in the bone china landscape.

Scott loves to be out on skis once again. He follows Gran with strong confident strides, skimming over the ice like a weightless insect over the surface of a pond, as they draw ever closer to Ponting's explosions of light.

'Unbelievable how bright!' shouts Gran to Scott.

'It would make a wonderful signal flare,' pants the captain, catching up to the Norwegian. 'Race you over there?'

One of the dogs is missing. Julick. It's been two weeks. Meares suspects he was set on by the other dogs, his frozen carcass buried somewhere under metres of fresh snow. Of course there's also the possibility that he fell through the ice. All the dogs roam free and they frequently track down seals, harassing them, mauling them to death. Chancing on half-eaten remains, a dark smudge of red on the ice, the men curse the dogs for wasting what would have fed the entire Cape Evans hut for a few days. At least slipping into the water through a crack in the ice is a quick death for a dog – no more than a few minutes. Still, Scott scans the landscape for any sign of the beast – another animal gone.

Gran easily outpaces his student. He is a national champion, after all. Sliding to a stop near Ponting's iceberg, Gran extends his hand to the captain.

'Not bad for a man of forty-three, eh?' grins Scott, clasping the Norwegian by the hand.

'Well done, sir!'

The men catch their breath. Scott turns his gaze south. The smile fades. 'I hate not knowing what's become of the Cape Crozier party.'

'Five weeks now, isn't it, sir?'

'Yes,' sighs Scott. 'Such fine men. Such dreadful weather. The conditions here over the last few weeks have been appalling, but Cape Crozier will have had it ten times worse.' Scott forces himself to look away. To instead focus on his upbeat Norwegian ski instructor. 'I'm being negative. Of course it's still too early to expect them. Come on, let's get back underway.'

Icebound. The *Terra Nova*'s journey southward turns into a
waiting game. Altogether it takes the ship three weeks to pass
through the pack.

While the dogs are eventually unchained, the ponies must see out the rough sea journey in their stalls.

Leads open up in the sea ice with the help of wind and sea currents but can just as quickly disappear.

Depot laying is a priority while summer conditions prevail. Men wearing snow goggles and reindeer gloves stack provisions around a central flag.

The Cape Evans hut sits on a beach of black lava overlooking McMurdo Sound. Scott is not entirely happy about the hut being a mere three and a half metres above the high tide mark.

Herbert Ponting, an experienced 'camera artist', has both a still camera and a movie camera to capture some of the first moving images of Antarctica and its wildlife.

Sea ice forming in the bay. Basking seals provide a plentiful supply of fresh meat for both men and dogs.

'The Tenements' – bunks belonging to Cherry-Garrard, Bowers, Oates, Meares and Atkinson.

Clissold's inventive repertoire includes seal liver curry and roast penguin breast. A saw and a hatchet are indispensable equipment in the Cape Evans kitchen.

Scott is the only man with his own room but it is far from luxurious with its narrow bunk, bookshelf and writing desk.

Apsley Cherry-Garrard is responsible for collating the many illustrations, poems and articles submitted anonymously to the *South Polar Times* during the long winter months.

Herbert Ponting is awed by his surroundings. Here he captures a dog team at rest, dwarfed by an iceberg that is trapped in the bay.

Titus Oates. Initially unimpressed with Scott, the cavalryman develops a healthy respect for the captain and is thrilled to be among the men chosen to accompany him on the polar journey.

Edgar Evans, or 'Taff' as he is affectionately known, had accompanied Scott to Antarctica during his *Discovery* expedition and impressed the captain with his strength and stamina.

Two sledges and over 340kg of gear to manhaul through the blackest night. The midwinter expedition to the Cape Crozier penguin colony is the first journey of its kind.

After surviving minus 54 degrees Celsius during their harrowing quest for penguin eggs, Wilson, Bowers and Cherry-Garrard enjoy their first meal back at Cape Evans.

Wilson with pony. While the ponies can haul heavy loads, they struggle in all but the most favorable snow conditions. However their meat will be vital to the men's survival.

Sledging rations include pemmican in a block, biscuits, sugar cubes, tea, butter and cocoa, delivering a total of 4200 calories – inadequate energy for manhauling a sledge.

The sledge dogs prove themselves to be efficient means of transport but unlike the ponies, are not fit for human consumption.

Finnesko boots – the reindeer skin boots provide both warmth and grip and remain soft and relatively easy to put on when left in subzero conditions overnight.

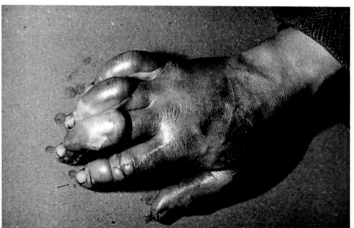

Dr Atkinson's hand is badly frostbitten after he becomes disorientated in a blizzard close by the Cape Evans hut.

One last group photo (minus Clissold who is laid up, and Ponting who is behind the camera). While 18 men will set out from Cape Evans, only five will make the final push to the south pole.

Maintaining momentum is key. Once it stops, the sledge becomes a deadweight and is extremely difficult to get going again. Each man is tethered separately for safety

Mt Erebus is seen in the background.

While primitive by today's standards, Scott's cotton, wool and fur items of clothing are waterproof, durable and insulating. Freedom of movement is also very important.

The desolation of defeat. There is little joy on the faces of Wilson, Bowers, Taff, Scott and Oates. Survival is now their principle aim.

CHAPTER TWENTY-SIX

'Spread out. Let them see there are three of us.' It's the first thing Wilson has said for hours. His teeth hurt. His feet are two numb blocks of meat. His back gives him so much pain, he fears it might crumble any minute. But Dr Wilson is happy.

The sight of the Cape Evans hut, huddled on the shore of McMurdo Sound with a coil of smoke issuing from its chimney, is more than Wilson, Bowers and Cherry-Garrard had ever hoped to see. They grind on, a shambling, ragged trio, shifting one frozen foot in front of the other with barely 1 kilometre to safety. Staying awake on their feet is no longer a problem.

Wilson says, 'I want to thank you two for what you have done. I couldn't have found two better companions.'

Nothing more needs to be said. The horror of what they have experienced cannot be expressed in words. Cherry clenches and unclenches his hands in his mitts, easing blood back into his fingers. The inside is thick with egg slime from when his penguin eggs broke. Caked onto the reindeer hide, the greasy protein of the egg sack has probably helped his hands survive the journey home. He longs to see his hands again. To wash off the egg slime. To be clean. It has been weeks.

As they near the hut, their thoughts turn to food, the impossible luxury of dry clothing and of a warm, dry bed. Bowers longs for a hot bath. Cherry, a slice of bread with jam.

'I think we might sleep outside for a time – just a day or two,' says Wilson.

'What?' Cherry's mouth drops. 'Outside? In the tent?'

'Give our systems a chance to acclimatise. Get back up to warmth gradually. It's not so cold here on the coast. It won't be too bad. We'll get ourselves some dry sleeping bags and some dry clothing, socks and mitts.'

Bowers seems unsure, 'Is that really necessary, Bill? My system's dying for a hot bath.'

'I fear the warmth of the hut will be a shock. Put unnecessary strain on our hearts, our compromised circulation. Our extremities might find it too much to bear.'

'I'm willing to give my extremities a shock,' says Bowers, glowering at Wilson. 'In the interests of science.'

The three men approach the hut in near silence. Not even the dogs stir. Carefully and for one last time, they help each other to struggle out of the harnesses. It seems quite unreal that they are finally home.

'No more pulling,' sighs Cherry. 'No more straining against this harness and sweating and . . .'

The door to the hut creaks open. It's Keohane. He's clearly heading out on the evening watch. 'Good God! It's the Crozier party,' he says, disappearing back into the hut.

'Well. That's a nice welcome!' snorts Bowers. 'Maybe I will sleep outside with you, Bill.'

A minute later, a whole crowd of men appear at the door with their breath coming in great welcoming clouds, as they cheer and laugh and clasp the three men by the shoulders. Scott can scarcely contain his joy. He's rushed outside in only a shirt.

'Welcome home, lads! It's such a relief to see you again. Come in. You need a hot meal and some fresh clothes. You certainly look like you could use both.'

Cherry and Bowers look at Wilson. But it's obvious that Uncle Bill is as desperate to take Scott up on his offer as the other two. He smiles at his travelling companions, 'After you,' he says gesturing at the open door.

Try as they might, the three men are unable to take off their clothing. Crean cuts it off their bodies with a pair of scissors. Gaunt and blackened from the smoke of their blubber stove, their faces look like charred remains. Their hair is matted and sticks to their heads. They haven't removed their balaclavas for almost six weeks. Ponting snaps away, ecstatic to capture their ravaged faces before they've had time to return to normal.

After dinner, the men take delight in weighing themselves and their sleeping bags. While each of them has lost body mass, their reindeer bags have more than doubled in weight – Cherry-Garrard's 8 kilogram bag contains more than 12 kilograms of ice.

'Imagine, dragging all that extra weight 100 kilometres for nothing,' he groans.

After a dinner of hot cocoa and enough bread and jam to satisfy their craving for something sweet, the men finally surrender to near-total exhaustion. Wilson, Bowers and Cherry slide easily into sleep. Nobody mentions the tent again. Their old beds are warm and dry.

CHAPTER TWENTY-SEVEN

'So, these penguin eggs – I hope you had some luck in that department?' Scott sits down at the table where Wilson and Cherry-Garrard are enjoying a rather late breakfast. There's a rule that any man not at the table by nine will miss out. But Scott has made an exception in this case – Wilson and Cherry have slept for twelve hours straight. Not so Bowers. He's been up for hours and is already back outside, helping launch one of Simpson's weather balloons.

'We have three,' Wilson smiles.

'Good,' says Scott. 'So we can say that your journey and all its hardship was worth it?'

Wilson glances at his breakfast companion. 'At least from my perspective. Cherry might have another view.'

'It was the worst journey in the world,' says Cherry, gulping back a mouthful of tea. 'And quite the best thing I've ever done in my life.'

'You know,' Wilson says quietly. 'I couldn't have done it without these two incredible men at my side. Even when we discovered that our tent had blown away and it looked like we would never return home, Bowers and Cherry had a smile and a song to keep our spirits up. Do you remember, Cherry, when we'd lost not only the tent but also our canvas roof? Birdie poked his head out of his sleeping bag after twenty-four hours of a howling blizzard and shouted, "Are we alright?"'

Cherry laughs at the memory. 'And we both shouted back, "We're alright!"'

'In actual fact, none of us were alright. But we weren't about to let on to the others!'

'Three whole days we huddled there in our bags, with the drift piling up around us and not a crumb to eat.'

'Or a hot drink to keep our engines going, to warm our feet and hands.'

Wilson's expression changes. 'By some miracle, Bowers found the missing tent. When the blizzard let up. It was on the slopes of Mt Terror, folded up neatly like an umbrella around the tent poles. After that lucky break, we all decided that heading home was the only option.'

Cherry looks up at Wilson. 'You know I thought I was going to die.'

'We all did, Cherry,' says Wilson a little sadly. His sense of responsibility for the other two men still weighs on his conscience.

'No, I mean I actually wanted to die. For it all to be over. We were so encrusted in ice and it was so dark and the wind was pounding us. We were falling asleep in our tracks, even mid-sentence we were so exhausted. We barely slept – we just kept on. Heading home. But all along I really did hope a crevasse would open up and take it all away.'

'It was dreadful, Robert,' says Wilson. 'Far worse than I had ever imagined. You know we nudged minus 54 one day?'

'We have much to learn from your experiences,' says Scott. 'You've all been to the limits of endurance. I'm desperate to hear from you about the suitability of your rations, your clothing and footwear and your camping equipment. Already I can see that we should consider airing the sleeping bags on the sledge to allow moisture to escape. Rolling them up tightly for travel.'

'Well, after a few days we couldn't roll them up as we did during our depot-laying journey,' says Wilson, his eyes wide with disbelief. 'They froze as rigid as an ironing board while we were in them. I tried to bend mine and the hide split.'

'These are all excellent lessons. As pleasant as spring conditions appear down here at Cape Evans, we can be sure that once we reach the Antarctic plateau, all of that will change. And we won't be a hundred miles from home, but a thousand.'

CHAPTER TWENTY-EIGHT

'Clissold, might I have a word?'

'Certainly, sir,' Clissold wipes the flour from his hands and follows Scott to his cubicle. The cook's heart is all aflutter. Has he done something wrong? Are his meals getting too bland? Or maybe too exciting? Perhaps the men have been secretly complaining about eating seal four times a week.

Scott clears his throat. 'We have all been exceedingly impressed by your skills as a cook these past months,' he says. 'The dedication you've shown in feeding these men a varied and imaginative diet is exemplary.'

'Thank you, sir.' Sweat prickles Clissold's brow.

'But your significant skill in all things mechanical has not escaped my notice either.'

'Thank you, sir. I used to be a mechanic, actually, before I enlisted in the navy. I like to tinker,' he says, smiling. 'I've tried to lend a hand when Day and Lashly need me.'

'Well, I wanted to ask you if you would consider accompanying us on our southern journey. We need as many hands as possible and a man with your skills to help with the two motor sledges would be a real asset.'

Clissold's mouth hangs open. His eyes dart around the room, as if waiting for Scott to tell him it's a joke. But Clissold is not so sure it is a joke. The cook licks his lips. 'You want me? To come with you?'

Scott's piercing blue eyes have not left Clissold. His eyes are not joking eyes. 'At least to help with getting everything across the Great Ice Barrier.'

'Very well . . .' Clissold says, his words slow and deliberate so as not to betray his excitement. He wonders if he should salute the captain. Or dance a jig. Or holler and whoop. Not once has he dreamed of taking part in the polar journey and now, to be asked by Scott himself – it's beyond belief.

Scott has been quietly considering all the men during the past months. Only a handful will join him on the

140

final stage. He's delighted at how well everyone has got on during their long winter confinement and impressed at how the Cape Crozier party drew the necessary strength from each other to overcome almost impossible conditions. He doubts whether he will come to any conclusion regarding the make-up of his final team before they depart. Perhaps not knowing if they've made the grade will ensure everyone works to the best of their ability. One thing is for sure – there are going to be some mightily disappointed fellows.

CHAPTER TWENTY-NINE

Daylight returns in a sweet rush. The motor sledges are out every fine day. Lashly and Clissold have made various modifications to the engines to ensure they will neither run too hot nor seize in the freezing temperatures on the Barrier. Scott is not at all sure the motor sledges are up to the task, but with only ten horses and twenty-three dogs, he's got to trust in every possible means of transport at his disposal. Most of the ponies are in good shape. They've benefited from increased exercise and rations since daylight has returned. At night they kick at the walls of their stalls, impatient to spend more time in the fresh air after their long winter in the blubber-stove fug of the stables.

Scott has allocated a pony to each of his men so that they can get to know the animal and its habits ahead of their departure. Oates's pony Christopher is particularly frisky, and fights regularly with the pony called Chinaman. Whenever he sees a chance, Christopher gallops away and has to have one of his forelegs tied up when Oates hitches him to the sledge. The pony must get into the habit of pulling to be of any use. Ever patient, Oates tries again and again. Murmuring soothing words to Christopher, Oates finally gets him to walk sedately with a modest load. His cooperation is short lived. Five minutes later he's had enough. He charges head on at Bowers and Keohane, in the hope that a collision with their ponies will rid him of his cumbersome sledge.

Ponting and Scott capture the scene on film, trying not to laugh as various men fling themselves at Christopher's sledge in an effort to slow the creature's mad dash.

'A true comedy,' says Ponting, always keen to catch the lighter side of Cape Evans life.

Scott turns his pale face to the sun and closes his eyes against the gauzy light that, as yet, holds little warmth. 'It changes the outlook, doesn't it, Herbert? Having the sun on your face and all that light beaming down.'

'Good for a photographer, too,' agrees Ponting. 'The landscape has come alive these last few weeks and I've got so much more I want to capture around Cape Evans.'

Scott follows Ponting's gaze. There's a great deal to take in, from the steam rising out of the summit of Mt Erebus, to the dark islands across the bay and the crimson bergs locked in the tight embrace of the sea ice. He scans the low foothills behind the hut to the distant mountain ranges to the west. Scott can't help but feel sorry for Amundsen and his men, who have had to endure the long winter on the featureless Barrier edge at the Bay of Whales. To wake every morning to the dreary white plain ahead of you and a slate-coloured sea at your back – they can't have ventured far from their hut. And judging by Wilson's report of poor weather at Cape Crozier, the Norwegians will have had a terrible time. Scott's thoughts turn to Amundsen's dogs, utterly exposed and buffeted all winter by ferocious polar blizzards. How many have perished? Have any survived?

'What's on your mind, Captain?' asks Ponting.

'I was just thinking how I shall be glad to get away and put our fortune to the test,' says Scott with passion. 'The trouble is, Herbert, I'm not so good at waiting.'

CHAPTER THIRTY

'Come on Clissold, that's a chap. Just a bit higher.' Ponting wriggles around slightly to get the angle right. 'Don't worry, those crampons will hold you.'

The berg juts out from the ice like a great white sphinx. The natural light is marvellous and Clissold has proven to be the perfect model, happy to pose for extended periods without the fiddling and impatient chatter of the other men Ponting has worked with.

The cook strikes a heroic pose. He wouldn't mind a copy of these snaps – to make his mum proud, to show off to his friends at the village pub. They show him right in the thick of the action, ice axe at the ready – not just up to his eyeballs in seal meat amid the pungent smells of the Cape Evans kitchen.

'Stay as you are,' calls Ponting. 'I'll just get a few shots from over here. With Erebus in the background.' Ponting trots away from the berg, humming to himself. This is going to be a wonderful series of photos.

'You alright, Thomas?' he shouts back as he focuses the shot.

'Yes!' comes the reply. Clissold gives a quarter turn towards the photographer and suddenly realises just how far he is from the ground. Vertigo sends him momentarily off balance, his feet lose purchase. His axe goes down to bite into the berg's backbone but the ice gives way. In a blink he's over the edge, sliding some distance over a rounded surface before plummeting down a 2 metre drop. With a loud *thwack* he lands, his back taking the full force of his fall on a sharp angle in the wall of the berg.

'Thomas!' yells Ponting. Clissold lies motionless on the snow. 'Thomas!'

'My back,' Clissold groans.

'I'll get help,' Ponting says, panic rising in his voice. 'You're going to be fine.'

'My back,' Clissold says again. His eyelids droop and close.

'I've killed Thomas,' howls Ponting. 'I've killed him.' Ponting stands up, thinks better of it, then shrinks back down beside Clissold. 'I must get help,' he tells himself, before shrieking: 'I've killed Thomas!'

Bowers, Atkinson and Scott are first on the scene. Ponting paces up and down in the background, wringing his hands and cursing himself for putting the young man in harm's way.

Clissold is out cold, but he's still alive. Carefully, the men slip him into a sleeping bag and load him onto a sledge.

Back at the hut, Wilson and Atkinson examine the patient, taking great care not to move him more than necessary. Luckily the young cook has regained consciousness, but judging by the confused nature of his speech, he is badly concussed.

'His head's had a dreadful whack,' says Wilson. 'He's talking complete gibberish. He keeps saying his mother is at the pub. He hasn't a clue where he is.'

Scott comes closer. Carefully he removes Clissold's glove and takes the cook's hand in his. 'Thomas, you've had a fall. You're fine now. Goodness knows you've given poor Ponting a fright but you're fine. Dr Atkinson and Dr Wilson have both had a good look at you. Rest is what you need.'

Clissold looks up at Scott, his eyes alert and searching, 'Is the sledging gear ready, sir?'

Scott frowns. He doesn't follow. He looks to Atkinson and Wilson.

'To the pole, sir. Are the sledges packed, sir? Are they ready to go?' Clissold asks again.

Wilson nods his head at the captain. For now, it's best to play along with the young man's delirium.

Scott gives the cook a sad smile. 'Yes, Clissold, they're packed and ready to go. Have yourself a rest and then you can join them.'

CHAPTER THIRTY-ONE

Scott has left on skis. Eager to get back into a sledging regime, he's taken Bowers, Taff, Evans and Simpson westward to the Ferrar Glacier. Charles Wright, the expedition's resident physicist, installed markers there the previous summer. The idea is to check the markers are still in place, taking measurements to work out how fast the glacier is moving. It's another important contribution to the scientific knowledge the expedition will be taking back to England and the world.

Pulling is easy with minimal provisions and equipment. Feeling fit and strong after winter, and knowing that they'll only be gone for a fortnight, the men are keen to push themselves. They even try to continue hauling their sledges during a blizzard. While it is possible, it's slow going, and when Simpson's face becomes badly frostbitten, Scott calls halt to the over-zealous experiment.

Back at Cape Evans, Gran is out on the ice posing for photos in his skis. Ponting has decided to avoid the more dramatic shots. Now he gets his subjects to pose on firm ground, suggesting action, not danger. The last thing he expects to see is a mangy dog rushing towards him, its tail wagging with enthusiasm.

'I think it's Julick,' says Gran.

Ponting puts down his camera just in time. The dog leaps at the photographer, its great paws leaving greasy stripes down his front as it seeks out any sign of human kindness. Ponting wrinkles his nose. 'Get down, you stinky beast!' he shrieks.

The dog's muzzle is encrusted with blood. A strong smell of seal blubber lingers on his thick coat.

Gran gives the dog a series of friendly slaps on his body. 'He seems fit and strong,' he says, puzzled. 'Where you been, Julick?' he asks. 'You been gone for so long.'

The dog just wags its tail and licks its lips. Ponting takes a photo for good measure. The last photo he took of this animal was at the end of last summer, when he set the gramophone up on the snow outside the hut.

The dogs loved it – howling while the soprano warbled out some operatic tune. Julick had come closest – no doubt curious to see the lady singer in the great wooden box.

The dog has been missing for more than a month. It seems strange that he should have only now found his way back home. The sounds of Cape Evans carry easily in calm weather – perhaps 10 kilometres or more. It's possible that he's been out at sea, cast adrift on a wedge of sea ice until favourable winds returned him to shore.

'Meares will be pleased,' says Ponting.

'Forget Meares,' says Gran. 'Scott will be overjoyed. He's got one more helper to get him to the pole.'

'Well, I heard he may have lost Jehu, Atkinson's pony – he's never recovered from the chill he got when he decided to swim ashore from the *Terra Nova*,' says Ponting.

'Chinaman is none too strong. And that James Pigg – he's not the world's healthiest specimen either,' adds Gran.

Ponting starts to pack up his gear. 'Thankfully Oates is tending to them. Did you hear how he cured the ponies of their mysterious skin irritation? Washed them down with water that had had tobacco soaking in it. Whatever the source of the ailment, it was gone in a few days.'

Oates has become well known for his careful preparation of the ponies in the weeks leading up to their departure. He intends to wrap the ponies' legs so sinking in the soft snow won't make them as cold. He's also improved their rugs – extending them further down their hind quarters so they will better withstand the wind when camping in the open. The ponies' bridles have received his attention, too. He's added fringing to protect their eyes from the glare of the summer sun. Scott values his contribution hugely.

Ponting nods thoughtfully. 'So much depends on those ponies. Oates is a dedicated man. A pessimist at heart, but one who can anticipate many troubles before they arise.'

'I wonder if he anticipated Amundsen?' asks Gran.

'I'm not sure anyone anticipated Amundsen – not even his own men.'

Both men fall silent.

Gran claps Ponting on the back. 'Let's get Julick home. Everyone will be pleased.'

'Yes,' agrees Ponting. 'At this point in time, we're all looking for a good omen.'

CHAPTER THIRTY-TWO

So much depends on the weather. The distance they will need to cover is 1200 kilometres. The journey will take months. But if Scott and his men cannot get to the pole and back during the relatively short summer season, their survival cannot be guaranteed.

There are three distinct stages to Scott's southern journey. The first part is crossing the Great Ice Barrier. The second is the ascent of the crevasse-riddled Beardmore Glacier. During the third stage of their journey, the men will march across the polar plateau, a vast, high-altitude plain, ravaged by winds. Only then will they reach 90 degrees south.

And, having achieved their goal, the men will then need to make the perilous trek home. With haste. Being out in the open and exposed to winter conditions is a death sentence, particularly for men who have had to push themselves to the brink both physically and mentally.

'Clissold, I'm afraid things have changed somewhat,' says Scott with sympathy. 'Your health remains our priority, and having spoken with both Dr Wilson and Dr Atkinson, I cannot foresee an instance where you will be well enough to accompany us on our outward journey.'

Clissold nods. He has guessed as much. While he has recovered from his head injury, his back is still fearfully sore. A walk of any distance is quite simply out of the question. The cook knows that only a few men will be chosen to make the last stage of the journey to the pole. And he also knows there's no chance of making the final cut. But to set out on the first stage of this epic journey with everyone else would have been enough of an honour.

'I realise that this will be an enormous disappointment to you,' Scott says. 'As it is to me. I genuinely looked forward to drawing on your expertise. We're expecting a lot from those motors.'

Clissold looks down and clears his throat. 'Well, I'm here at least, on the *Terra Nova* expedition. That in itself is something to tell my grandchildren – the year I spent feeding up the world's most famous polar explorer and all the men who made his dash to the pole possible.'

Scott can't help but smile at Clissold's compliment. He'd dearly love to be the world's most famous explorer. But he's not yet. He has many miles to cover before he can lay claim to that honour.

The motors head off that afternoon. Without Clissold. Without great hopes. The motors held such promise. Exceedingly expensive, they were the expedition's secret weapon. But Scott has seen enough of their lacklustre performance to know it was all a dream. He's seen their limitations, how their rollers shred and slip on the ice, failing to grip. It will be a good thing if Lieutenant Evans, Lashly and Day can get more than a few days out of their slow grind. At least they'll shoulder some of the weight of provisions, and save the ponies a few days' hard slog.

Four days later, the pony teams set off – a great rambling cavalcade heading out to Hut Point, where Ponting is waiting with Meares, Dimitri and the two dog teams to capture on film the departure of the brave party, their animals and sledges piled high, trekking into the unknown to conquer the South Pole for the honour of king and country.

'Where's the Union Jack?' asks Scott suddenly.

'We can't possibly be photographed without our esteemed flag,' says Wilson.

'Bowers?' asks Scott. 'Any idea where we might have packed it?'

'Sir, I completely forgot to bring it.'

'You realise we'll need it where we are going, don't you?' Wilson says, laughing. 'It may not nourish us, shelter us or keep our feet warm and dry, but the Union Jack is the reason we are attempting this bold journey. I suggest we get our very fastest man to return at once to Cape Evans and fetch it.'

The fastest man is undoubtedly Gran. The champion skier returns with the flag a short time later. With a look of great reverence, the young Norwegian hands the carefully folded Union Jack to Captain Scott. Everyone knows how desperately Gran wants the captain to succeed, to beat Amundsen in his audacious plan to steal the pole. Yet everyone knows that the Norwegians, with their many Siberian huskies, may already be on their way, with only tragedy or misfortune to forestall their swift progress.

'I wish you godspeed, Captain,' says Gran.

Scott is touched by the young man's loyalty. He wants Gran to know that he does not hold any ill will towards him or his countrymen. 'You're young. You've got your whole life before you. Take care of yourself. God bless you.'

It is a fine blessing, bestowed on him by a man he greatly admires. Even so, Gran watches his hero go with a heavy heart.

CHAPTER THIRTY-THREE

The ponies follow the straight tracks left by the motor sledge party. Michael and Victor speed ahead. Snatcher at a gallop. Christopher is misbehaving as usual. Snippets and Bones are steady as ever. Nobby, as obstinate as usual. Chinaman and James Pigg are dawdling, but make progress. And Jehu brings up the rear. Atkinson is leading him slowly, not wanting to overtax the scrawny pony, who he is hoping will provide a few days of hard work. Then again, it's a minor miracle that the pony made it as far as Hut Point.

All the ponies are off their food, although Bones happily eats Christopher's protective fringe from his bridle when the animals are tethered together at their first camp. The midnight sun is bright and warm but the air temperature is cold, and when the wind picks up and whips loose snow into the air, the glare is intense. With eyes exposed to the splinters of light, Christopher is sure to suffer snow blindness and give Oates even more trouble. Overall, the ponies seem to be coping better with the snow conditions than during depot laying. Of course their loads are much lighter this time around, thanks to the motors. Scott decides to march at night and give the ponies a chance to rest in the warmth of the daytime as they did last summer.

Lieutenant Evans and Day have left a note on an abandoned petrol canister. It reads:

Going well. We passed here on 28th October at 9pm.

Another note a bit further simply says:

Cylinder trouble.

After another few kilometres, the men make out the dark lump on the horizon. It's one of the motors – abandoned.

'The tracks lead forward,' says Scott. 'We have one of the motors still functional, at least.' He has no doubt they'll soon come across the last remaining motor sledge, smoking and spent. Sure enough, on the fifth day of their march across the Barrier they spy three black dots in the vast white landscape. The motor and the two sledges it has been hauling. As previously agreed, Evans, Day, Hooper and Lashly will now continue to manhaul the sledges themselves.

Christopher is proving a real nuisance. It takes four strong men to hitch him to his sledge. Even then he will try every trick to escape the harness, flinging his head around, kicking wildly, even lying down. The first 10 kilometres are murder for Oates's arm, which feels like it will be wrenched from its socket until finally the pony's bad humour wears off. With all the hassle of setting out, Oates is very reluctant to stop part way through their day's march for any reason – even lunch. Oates decides to push the pony onwards, only calling a halt for the evening camp. It's troubling that the ponies are not eating their forage. With all the hard work of pulling in deep snow, the ponies need to eat or they'll become weaker as each day passes. Despite their lack of appetite, they seem to need a lot of water, stopping regularly in their march to gobble mouthfuls of snow.

Strange clouds clutter the sky. The sun's brightness is swallowed by a gloom that stretches far and wide. The temperature rises.

'The sky's lowering,' says Scott to Wilson. 'Unsettled.'

'Do you think we're in for a blizzard?' asks Wilson.

'Undoubtedly. Let's stop now and do everything we can to shelter the ponies.'

But there's no way to keep the ponies comfortable. Even with their improved pony blankets, the poor animals freeze as fine particles of snow are blown deep into their furry coats, where they melt in contact with the skin.

'That snow's coming thick and fast,' Bowers says, struggling into the tent. 'We've built up some walls to protect them from the worst of the blow but the drift is fast rising up their legs. The sledges are thoroughly covered.'

'This weather will sap the strength of those beasts,' says Scott. 'So much of our plan depends on their continued wellbeing.'

Oates has plenty of advice. 'Of all things, the most important for horses is that conditions should be placid while they stand tethered.'

'Well, I'm afraid that's a little out of my control at present,' says Scott, annoyed.

'I know that, sir,' says Oates. 'I'm just warning you that you'll struggle to get your required 16 kilometres out of them if they have too much of this. And as for those crocks – Chinaman and Jehu – they'll struggle to get through the night.'

After a night of wakeful worry, Scott orders the men to break camp. Conditions have improved slightly and Chinaman and Jehu are not only alive, but eager to move off with their slightly lighter loads. By lunchtime the wind has dropped and the sun has reappeared through broken clouds, although the ponies must still contend with a strong headwind.

Out on the Ice Barrier, not only do the weather conditions change rapidly, but the quality of the surface can go from bad to worse to passable in the space of a few hours. The sastrugi offer particularly challenging terrain. Irregular waves of wind-hardened snow, sometimes half a metre in height, they make heavy going. Navigating the soft snow that gathers in the dips between the sastrugi is a challenge of another kind.

The ponies trudge on, now travelling in three distinct groups – the stragglers who set out first, followed by the medium-paced ponies, and finally the fliers. The dogs leave well after everybody else and trot happily through the 16 kilometres that the ponies are urged to cover. Seemingly unaffected by the weather, they could easily double that distance. Working as they are, the dogs have developed healthy appetites. Knowing this, Meares keeps a close eye on Jehu and Chinaman, quietly hoping his dogs are only a matter of days from a good feed.

CHAPTER THIRTY-FOUR

One Ton Depot. It doesn't seem long ago that they were here, hurrying to offload their final supply cache in order to get the failing ponies back to Cape Evans. They've covered a little over 200 kilometres. It has taken a full two weeks to struggle along this far, heaving the ponies back to their feet whenever the animals get stuck, sweating as they free up the frozen metal runners in knee-deep snow, righting upturned sledges, ploughing on towards the horizon.

Scott orders a day's rest. While he is happy with their progress, Scott worries constantly about the condition of the ponies. Victor is looking gaunt. Jehu has maybe one more day in him. The deep, soft snow is a bad enough drain on their limited physical resources, but the unseasonal weather is weakening them further. A thermometer left at the depot at the end of last summer has registered a minimum temperature of minus 58 degrees Celsius. The oats that Scott scattered for Simpson at the same time to show wind direction has totally disappeared, its contents either blown away or buried.

Their surroundings are shrouded in a thick mist when they set off again. When everything is blankly white and the sky and the land merge into one, it becomes increasingly difficult to keep perspective. The ponies struggle in such conditions. With no landmarks or points of reference to walk towards, the men also feel a deep sense of claustrophobia and isolation. Most men wear goggles of green tinted glass to cut out the glare and increase definition, although on days of walking into white blankness there is nothing to see apart from the ghostly tracks of the preceding sledge disappearing into the mist. Bowers is convinced he sees what looks like a herd of cattle in the distance. He laughs when he realises he's fallen victim to an optical illusion. His herd of cattle is nothing but scattered pony dung.

On 21 November, some three weeks after leaving Cape Evans, Scott and his team catch up to Lieutenant Evans and the men who abandoned the motor sledges and have been manhauling ever since. Scott's second-in-command and his companions have been waiting at their agreed rendezvous spot for six days. In spite of their ample rest, the men are hungry after pulling through deep drifts for several weeks. Hooper and Day will now head home, leaving Evans and Lashly to continue with new, fresher sledging mates.

'A word, Captain?' Meares asks.

'Certainly Meares, what can I do for you?' Scott asks, although he has a pretty good idea what the frustrated dog driver wants.

'My dogs need a feed. They're getting ravenous.'

Scott nods. 'You've been asking every day, Meares. And every day I've held off. That Jehu has turned into a real champion – our very own 'Barrier Warrior'. I realise his days are numbered but every day he seems to find the courage to move on again. I really do feel he could do another three marches. Atkinson believes so, too.'

Meares sighs, failing to hide his frustration. 'My dogs can carry the extra weight, sir. As long as they can get a decent feed. If not, I'm afraid we'll start to see their condition suffer.'

'The harder snow is good for the ponies but the sledges don't slide so easily over it,' Scott thinks aloud. 'Perhaps we are better to sacrifice poor old Jehu for the dogs; they are proving to be good pullers.'

Scott has another worry. The forage, the only food sustaining the ponies, will eventually run out. He never dreamed Jehu and Chinaman would make it this far – a full eight marches beyond One Ton Depot. His plan is to get at least some of the ponies to the bottom of the Beardmore Glacier, 240 kilometres away. He knows the forage will not last that long with this number of them.

There is a cold wind blowing when Meares leads Jehu back along the track. It's a merciful end to his life. Quick and painless, the bullet passes into his skull. The pony's body folds over heavily onto the snow. After the other ponies have left the camp, Meares and Dimitri set to work; there's a lot of fat left on the pony and Meares thinks there will be enough meat for at least four feeds for his hungry dogs.

'I cannot wait to see them get into this meat,' smiles the Russian dog handler. 'They can smell it.'

'Make sure you keep some aside, Dimitri,' says Meares, cleaning his knife on the snow. 'There are a few men that wouldn't mind their fair share of Jehu as well.'

CHAPTER THIRTY-FIVE

The remaining ponies lurch forward, dragging their impossible loads through the endless waves of wind-hardened snow. The surface crust collapses underfoot with a boom and a rumble like shellfire from a distant battlefield.

Nobby and Bones remain the strongest pullers. Victor and Christopher are the weakest. It's been several days since Jehu and, some days later, Chinaman were shot and carved up for the dogs. Pony meat and pemmican is on the menu in all the tents. With limited fuel supplies, the men can't afford to cook it for long. The meat is semi-raw and terribly tough.

'A year's care and good feeding,' says Bowers, stirring the pot. 'Three weeks' work with good treatment, a reasonable load and good ration, and then a painless end. If anybody can call that cruel I cannot either understand it or agree with them.'

'You might feel differently when Victor ends up in the stew,' says Cherry-Garrard.

Bowers shrugs. 'We'll cross that bridge when we come to it.' He's surprised that others have noticed how fond he's grown of his travelling companion, even sharing a biscuit with him at mealtimes. On the sly, of course.

Everyone is suffering during the marches. The men sink to their shins and the ponies leave holes a foot deep. Even on skis the going is tough. When snow is falling thick as a hedge they cannot slow their pace. They must pick up at least 20 kilometres if they are to reach the foot of the glacier as hoped.

'Seven marches to go until we get to the glacier, Oates,' says Scott. 'How are we looking?'

'Four bags of forage left,' Oates grunts in reply. He's sick of Scott's constant questions. It's nothing but fussing as far as he's concerned. The ponies will last as long as they have to.

Scott's timetable is very much guided by Ernest Shackleton's progress in 1909, when he forged inland with a small team of men and ponies, hoping to reach the pole. Scott pores over Shackleton's diaries, comparing distances, weather and snowfall. While they haven't lost a day's march yet, Scott's men have already fallen behind Shackleton's schedule. They just can't seem to make up the daily distances. The conditions are to blame – not the men. Where Scott has experienced deep snow and horrible weather, Shackleton enjoyed sun and pleasant summer conditions. As December approaches, the best month for travel, Scott can only hope that their luck will turn.

Oates is still grumbling: 'The truth of the matter is, the ponies will outlast their forage. We must keep sacrificing the ponies – even the ones that aren't failing.'

Scott sighs. 'We could really get through now with the dogs' help and without much delay, yet every consideration makes it desirable to save men from heavy hauling as long as possible.'

As tough a time as the ponies are having, the manhauling team has it worse. They leave a full two hours before the rest of the party but have totally lost their lead by lunchtime. Lieutenant Evans is an excellent skier, having worked hard with Gran to build his skills over the months at Cape Evans. As second-in-command he knows he must prove himself. He's determined to be one of the men Scott chooses for the pole. He sets a cracking pace for both Atkinson and Lashly, and keeps the mental strain of navigating in the dismal conditions to himself. They're all suffering. In silence. Complaining loudly about how hard it is to pick a course through the blank wall of white will achieve little.

By the beginning of December, land has appeared. Scott stops to take photos of the massive, rounded mountains appearing from the mist with a delicate branching pattern of snow and ice starkly visible against black cliffs of exposed rock.

They make camp, relieved that the monotony of the Barrier is mostly behind them. Christopher must go. Nobody is particularly sad at the prospect of losing the most troublesome pony that ever lived, although Oates insists that he must do the deed. True to character, Christopher is a most uncooperative victim. He jerks his head away just as Oates pulls the trigger. The bullet whizzes past the pony's head and sends the animal flying about the camp in a mad panic, upturning sledges, pulling out tent ropes and sending men diving for cover.

Victor's death is a quiet affair by comparison. Bowers bids farewell to his travelling mate, feeds him one last biscuit and sets to work offloading a sledge. He closes his eyes on hearing the gunshot.

CHAPTER THIRTY-SIX

It should be beautiful. A sight of pure loveliness – a picture from a Christmas card or a fairytale. A winter wonderland. But to Scott's eyes, the scene outside his tent is beastly. The snow cascades from the sky, obliterating even the neighbouring tents in its abundance. The snowflakes are lavish. Luxurious in size. Great pompoms of vileness, they sweep around the tent.

'Our luck is preposterous,' says Scott through gritted teeth. 'This is the greatest snowfall I have known in summer. Ever!'

The snow drums on the canvas of the tent. So close to the Beardmore Glacier, and the end of the first stage of their journey, and they're in the midst of a full-blown blizzard. They are unable to advance an inch. The temperature has risen to zero. The snow sticks to everything, melting the second it touches any surface. The drifts cover the sledges, reach more than halfway up the side of the tents. To be outside for one or two minutes is to be covered entirely from head to toe. The ponies are up to their bellies. Any part of their bodies not covered by a rug – head, tail, legs – is encrusted in ice.

'Do you think it's a bad season, Bill? Is there some atmospheric disturbance? Is it like this everywhere, or have we been singled out for exceptional local conditions?'

Wilson frowns. He doesn't answer. He knows what Scott is getting at. Amundsen. Is he getting this weather too?

'Here we are, our small party getting all the bad weather in one place while the others have probably got only sunshine.' Scott is beginning to rant. His frustration is boiling over.

'There's no way of knowing what conditions the Norwegians are facing. They may have it worse than us.'

Scott doesn't seem to hear his friend's words. 'Nothing could prepare us for this. No foresight, no preparations. This is so unfair!'

Oates appears at the entrance to the tent. The man is soaking wet, like he's just walked through a rain shower, not a snow storm. 'The pony wall blew down. We'll need men to repair it,' he says loudly. 'I'll get Taff and Cherry and Crean.'

'I'll go too,' says Keohane, struggling out of his sodden sleeping bag and back into his wet outdoor clothing. He's sick of lying flat. Time for fresh air and a fresh soaking.

Whether they're outside in the snow or inside the tent, they're equally waterlogged. The tent itself is wet through and through. Water pools on their sleeping bags, their personal belongings and their finneskos.

'If a cold snap should follow on the heels of this tropical downpour,' says Wilson. 'And we fail to dry everything out, serious trouble will be had by all. Believe me, it becomes extremely difficult to move when the body is encased in ice.'

Before he leaves, Keohane hands Scott a piece of paper. 'To cheer you up, sir,' he says.

Scott unfolds it, reads it, then gives in to laughter. 'Listen to this, Bill,' he says.

> *The snow is melting and everything is afloat,*
> *If this goes on much longer we shall have to turn the tent over,*
> *And use it as a boat.'*

'Thank the Lord for our companions,' says Wilson. 'Their good humour will see us through until the very end.'

But there is no end in sight. After three days confined to the tents, shivering in wet clothes that cling to the skin, the men are feeling desperate. The camp is devoid of laughter. There is none of the usual cheer at mealtimes. Instead, the men watch the water dribble down the tent poles.

Scott has made ample provision for bad weather in his planning, but according to his schedule, they should have commenced on the second stage of their journey. Already it's necessary to start on the Beardmore Glacier rations. The ponies themselves have only one small feed remaining. The animals will not starve – Scott is adamant. To subject them to anything that could be described as prolonged suffering is unacceptable. If they cannot march in the morning, the ponies will have to be shot, every single one of them.

On the fourth day, the wind drops. Scott rallies his dispirited troops.

'Men, I know conditions are still bad, but we need to dig out the sledges. And move the tents,' he says – they have all but disappeared into wet, icy holes. 'Lieutenant Evans: I want you and your men to try and pull a load.'

Lieutenant Evans, Lashly and Day are happy to harness up. But pulling a sledge through deep, wet snow the consistency of cold mashed potato proves impossible. They sink to their knees. They strap Nobby into the traces. He's the strongest of the ponies and their best hope. But the unfortunate creature bucks about on the spot, unable to shift the sledge. With snow up to his belly, he makes no progress at all.

'I think the ponies are finished,' says Wilson.

'Oates, what do you think?' Scott asks.

'If we get a change in the weather, they might have one more march in them, sir.'

'Without feed?' Scott looks doubtfully at Oates.

Oates shrugs his shoulders. 'There's a bit still left in their nose bags. I wouldn't call it a feed but it's something.'

Scott shakes his head.

'You either need them or you don't, sir,' says Oates. 'Either way, they're dead.'

Shambles Camp they call it. It's a fitting name for the place where the remaining ponies meet their end. The job's done quickly and without any sentimentality. Nevertheless, Scott chooses to walk some distance from camp. The shots ring out across the empty plain they have spent an eternity crossing. The animals, so steadfast, so necessary to Scott's longed-for victory, now lie motionless in the tainted snow.

Meares and Dimitri carve up the meat. Some will go to the dogs. Much of it will be buried in the snow for safekeeping. The men will no doubt need it when they pass through on their return journey. It's hot, heavy, messy work. Meares mutters at the foulness of the job, at the sheer volume of meat he must butcher. Soon the camp is indeed a shambles.

CHAPTER THIRTY-SEVEN

Almost 200 kilometres long and a full 2700 metres in height, the Beardmore Glacier is a daunting foe. Meares and Dimitri have gone on ahead with their last remaining dogs but their objective is limited. They will lay one last depot for the three teams of manhaulers before turning around and making for home. The glacier is no place for the animals.

So far, the dogs have fared well. The generous feeds of fresh meat at Shambles Camp, where the remaining ponies were shot, have had a good effect. They could trot on for many more weeks, but for the danger of crevasses. Scott remembers all too clearly the dramatic rescue at the end of last summer.

The howling creatures hanging in the void, the two lucky ones he was able to retrieve from the icy depths. Shackleton lost his one remaining pony on the Beardmore, in a crevasse so deep that the poor beast disappeared without a trace. It is far safer to manhaul their loads from now on. A man with even limited experience can generally tell if there's a disturbance or a change in the quality of the surface. Perils beneath the snow can often be accurately predicted by keeping alert. In any case, tethered individually to the sledge, a man who falls through the surface can be more easily rescued than a pack of howling, biting dogs.

The four-day blizzard on the Barrier has nudged an entire season of snowfall up the glacier. Skis allow the men to make some progress over the soft surface, but they aren't well suited to the steeper slopes ahead of them. Feet, legs are needed to push further up to where they will find a firmer, hard-packed surface. But when they take their skis off, the men sink up to the knees.

'Lord have mercy!' Taff cries out. 'I'm going to drown.'

The loads have been rearranged. Each of the sledge runners has been scraped free of ice and dried off. Anything is worth getting a better glide. But their weight is such that the sledges sink to their crossbars. Hauling in such conditions is exhausting. Like it or not, Scott and his men are ploughing the snow.

'Shackleton found hard blue ice here,' says Scott to his three sledge mates. Wilson, Oates and Taff are great pullers, and together they manage to get into a rhythm, swinging from side to side. Three kilometres an hour is the pace they manage to maintain. The going is easier once the sledge has been coaxed along and is moving. Maintaining momentum above everything else is the key. Once it stops, any sledge becomes a dead weight and unbearably hard to shift. When the sledge sinks in a particularly soft patch, the men have learnt to pull with a sideways action, heaving with their skis to free up the cumbersome load and get it on the move again.

'We might have to consider working as one team – to relay the sledges,' says Scott after several long days.

Wilson's heart sinks at the mention of relaying. He did more than his fair share during his Cape Crozier escapade. There's nothing more dispiriting than covering the same distance three times. 'Let's not give up just yet. The wind will harden the snow as we get higher, you'll see,' he says.

Lieutenant Evans and his team are drained. They fall a long way behind. It takes them several hours to cover a distance of a few hundred metres. His team has been manhauling since the motor sledges died. They have also been the trail blazers, setting the course for the entire party for more than a month. The strain is evident. Lieutenant

Evans is determined, but he's also suffering from snow blindness, as are Lashly, Bowers, Oates and Keohane. It's his own fault, he knows it. A total lack of caution. With all this heavy pulling, the goggles fog up almost immediately. Nobody can afford to stop their pulling to wipe them. They're an annoyance. But a necessary one.

With his burning eyes hidden under a loosely knotted handkerchief and his harness cutting into his chest, Evans allows his thoughts to wander to the little silk flag his wife gave him to leave at the pole. *Oh, the glory that awaits them!* 'Come on chaps, let's get this load of bricks to the top,' he says.

His sledge mates have had enough of his banter, his forced frivolity. It's all a show. A theatrical performance to demonstrate to Scott how splendidly his second-in-command is doing. They want to throttle him. Wright would like to push him down a crevasse and leave him chirping to himself while they move on at speed.

Snow blindness is not the only disadvantage of marching during the day. This is the time when the sun's rays are at their most powerful. Stripped down to their singlets, the men suffer sunburnt shoulders, faces and arms. Their lips are fried and covered in agonising blisters. The high temperatures also wreak havoc on the efficiency of the sledge runners, which melt the snow, then gather ice in hard spikes. There's little they can do. Every hundred metres or so, they must halt and clear the runners, scraping the ice with the back of a knife. It's a vital task but also a drain on precious time.

The sledge meters prove hopeless. It's anybody's guess how far they've come, and exactly how much further they must go. Every day is an epic struggle, wading through knee-deep clag. Every yard is a hard-won victory. Every crevasse they pass over safely is a minor miracle. They've all taken a tumble at one point or another, and thankfully nobody has been badly injured.

There were suggestions that snow conditions would improve with altitude. But having achieved 450 metres in vertical distance, the men find pulling conditions not easier but much harder. Snow cannot gather on the steep rocky faces on either side of the glacier. Funnelled by the wind into the glacier valley, vast volumes of snow become a sea. It is like a bad dream, when legs work furiously but make no headway.

Day after day the men do battle. They spend their days breathless and soaked in perspiration and their nights awake and uncomfortable, encased in clammy clothes and fighting off cramp in overworked muscles. More than a few endure bouts of painful indigestion. They double over with gut ache, their bowels tangled in spasms. Mostly they crave water. Out on the march, they'd give anything to satisfy their raging thirst – even a day's rations. The easiest thing would be to suck on a handful of snow. But any relief would be short-lived. Not only would they lose more energy melting the snow, leading to more severe dehydration, but their core temperature would drop significantly, introducing the prospect of hypothermia.

'Evans, I think it would be a good thing if we could take some of the weight from your sledge tomorrow and transfer it to ours,' Scott says at the end of the day. He can no longer hide his impatience at the slow progress of Evans's team. It's been most disappointing. After all, Evans has had Lashly, who is one of the strongest men, and Wright, who Scott knows has taken to sledging like a duck to water.

Lieutenant Evans licks his cracked lips even though he knows it will make them feel worse. 'No thank you, sir. It's a kind offer but one we must refuse. You have your own load to consider and we will manage with ours just as we have for some time now.'

'Your team is falling behind, Evans. And I fear you may hold us all back. It's the sixteenth of December and we are a full six days behind Shackleton, according to his schedule. We must make up distance if our provisions are to last.'

'Then we will pull harder, won't we chaps?' Evans smiles awkwardly at his team. They fail to smile back.

'In that case,' says Scott. 'I shall swap sledges with Bowers's team. It would appear that the one we've been hauling is slightly easier than theirs.'

The following morning, Scott, Wilson, Oates and Taff charge on up the hill, swinging in time like a clockwork soldier. Bowers, Cherry, Keohane and Crean find their new sledge every bit as heavy as the one they surrendered to Scott.

Bowers has covered his goggles with plaster to cut down the glare. He has the merest slit to peer from, far narrower than a letter box. He can see the tips of his skis and little else. His eyes still water. Perhaps it's the effort, the ten to fifteen desperate jerks they must give to get the sledge moving. He's never pulled so hard. The force crushes his insides. Bowers lets out a guttural roar and they're finally on their way. It doesn't help to see Scott and his team ahead of them, already small enough to fit within the confines of his goggle slit. Bowers knows that he and the other team haven't a hope of matching Scott's pace. They won't see him at lunch. Although they should see them at the evening camp, a full nine and a half hours later.

In spite of not being able to keep up with Scott's cracking speed, Bowers has little to fear. Scott has long admired the pluck and energy of Birdie Bowers. The captain knows him to be extremely capable, a rare fellow who shows no sign of pride or moodiness. Since returning from their

Cape Crozier journey, Wilson and Cherry-Garrard have shared many stories about Bowers's brave and selfless deeds in the direst conditions. It only serves to reinforce what Scott already knows. He will want Birdie with him at the pole.

CHAPTER THIRTY-EIGHT

Finally, blue ice underfoot. Pulling is easier; crevasses appear as obvious cracks. For the first time in a long while, the men can forge ahead with confidence. They've all experienced heart-stopping falls on the glacier. Cherry and Lieutenant Evans worst of all. Each of them knows that falling to the length of a sledging harness is to glimpse death.

On their feet they wear the crampons that Taff has fashioned for each member of the party over the winter months. The metal bites into the ice and provides the men with solid footing. It's a pleasing sensation after so many long weeks of wading through deep snow.

A wind keeps them pleasantly cool on their march and dries their clothes out. Heading onto the cold and wind-swept summit plateau, they cannot afford to be wet. As they near 1800 metres, their thoughts turn to the final stage of their journey and, in particular, who Scott will choose to go with him. It is a day they all dread, Scott most of all.

Throughout their ascent of the Beardmore Glacier, they've looked for any sign of the Norwegians. As the only known point of access to the summit plateau, the glacier seems the logical route for Amundsen to take. It seems strange that there should be neither dog tracks nor any signs of abandoned camp sites.

Despite the enormous physical effort that their ascent has required of them, and even with the pole in their sights, the men do not neglect their scientific endeavours. Bowers and Lieutenant Evans have been taking angles and observations at each stop. By the end of their uphill journey, they should have the first ever accurate survey of the glacier. Wilson has been making pencil drawings of rock faces and formations along the way to help identify the geological features of the area. It pleases Scott to be surrounded by such diligent men, but he knows that the greatest reward for their diligence will be reaching the South Pole. If Scott and his party can lay claim to that prize, the considerable scientific work that has been carried out during the *Terra Nova* expedition will be all the more valued by the world. Should he not succeed in his goal, the scientific work of Simpson, Wright, Debenham, Atkinson, Wilson and Taylor may well be overlooked or even forgotten by history.

As the party nears the very top of the glacier, they must go up and down many steep slopes. Each time the men get to the top of a ridge, they find another one beyond it. It is tiring work, not least because the sledges are hard to control on the downward slope and frequently outrun the haulers. Scott presses on and on up each ridge, powering on to the next until well into the evening. He is a man possessed, a man trying hard to outrun his thoughts.

'Cherry,' says Scott that night at camp. 'I'm afraid I have a blow for you.'

Cherry has been busily adjusting his skis in preparation for the next day's march. His heart sinks. He doesn't even need to hear what the leader has to say.

'I'm afraid I shall be sending you back tomorrow night. To Cape Evans.'

Cherry gives a nod, his eyes fixed on the ground as the terrible news sinks in.

Scott continues, 'I think it is especially hard on you – my decision. You've pushed yourself at every step of our journey. And it's been tough.'

Cherry gets to his feet. 'I hope I have not disappointed you.'

'No – no – no.'

Cherry manages a smile. 'I'm pleased to have made it this far. Remember how I failed my medical back in London? How the doctors told you I was half blind and would be a danger to myself and to others on such an ambitious expedition?'

'Yes,' Scott says, laughing. 'And I'm glad I didn't heed their advice. You have proved yourself time and again to be a splendid member of the expedition and a most able manhauler these past weeks.'

Cherry can't help but ask, 'Who else? Being sent back, I mean.'

'Atkinson, Wright and Keohane will also go back. I've asked Wright to navigate.'

'I see,' says Cherry. 'And Lieutenant Evans is staying on?'

'For the moment, yes. Wilson, Oates, Bowers, Taff, Crean and Lashly will remain, too, until I decide who will make the final push.'

Cherry must go and see Wright. He will be furious at the turn of events. Not to have made the grade and for Scott to have chosen the prideful Lieutenant Evans instead – Wright is sure to take it as an insult, proof that he should have pushed Scott's second-in-command down a crevasse when he had a chance.

CHAPTER THIRTY-NINE

The two sledging teams are 2400 metres above sea level and 455 kilometres from the pole. The eight men must clear the upper glacier icefalls as well as navigate a particularly nasty area where the crevasses are as wide as streets.

Scott leads. He does not have a map and he's not entirely sure where he's going. Striking out in one direction could easily lead the men into a dead-end situation. But using his knowledge of ice formations, Scott is confident of finding a more manageable route than the one Shackleton describes in his journals. The terrain is complex, a jumbled mess of rock and ice, elevations and depressions. For now, they must head west, but in their hearts, they all want to continue south.

With the enthusiasm that comes of having been chosen to come this far, the men pull well throughout the day. And despite each man taking a tumble into a crevasse (some more than once) both sledging teams make extremely good progress. They've also got very fast at breaking camp, reloading the sledges and getting in and out of their harnesses. Bowers is the only man who refuses skis. His short legs pound up and down like iron pistons, never failing, never falling behind.

Oates doesn't show it, but his feet are starting to give him trouble. They've been wet since setting out from Hut Point, and the repeated freezing and refreezing of his toes as he trudges on cannot be good. Also, the back tendon on his right leg feels like it has stretched out of shape. His mind travels back to the Cape Evans stable. What were Taff's words? *Scott won't want men who complain when they're cold, when they're hungry, when their feet go blue and they start pissing ice cubes.*

So Oates says nothing and his pace does not suffer. He's sure that everybody on the march has similar difficulties. Why be the fool that acknowledges his own?

'For the first time, our goal seems in sight,' says Scott to his sledging companions as they wait for the other team to haul Lashly from the jaws of a crevasse. 'We can pull these loads faster and farther than I had hoped. I only pray for good weather. We've got good clothes, we're well fed – we can stick a lot more.'

Conditions aren't perfect. The men are all wearing their wind blouses and head protection as they continue steadily climbing onto the summit plateau. The wind has picked up. They'd all hoped that, having left the glacier, the likelihood of crevasses was decreasing, but Lashly has proven them wrong. He must have fallen in a good distance. Usually when they fall, the men can scramble out by themselves without even stalling the sledge's advance. But this rescue effort is taking longer than usual.

'Poor blighter,' says Taff. 'To fall into a crevasse on your birthday . . . it's not quite the surprise you're looking forward to, is it?'

'I wish they'd hurry up,' says Oates. 'I'm fairly freezing in this wind.'

'Do you suppose he's alright?' asks Wilson. 'Perhaps we should backtrack.'

Scott says, 'They'd have signaled for us to come over if they needed our help. I think it's more likely that the angle is awkward or the edge unstable. Some of these crevasses have rather rotten sides. But I wish they'd hurry.'

After the cracking pace they've set, the men are only a couple of days behind Shackleton's schedule now. But Scott is forever anxious. It's Christmas Day already and there is still a phenomenal distance to cover. He thinks back to the interview he did with one of the London newspapers before he left. He'd suggested 22 December as an approximate date for reaching the pole. He wonders if Amundsen had that date in mind. If only that Norwegian had not turned this journey into a race, he'd be a good deal more relaxed. He knows the team have it in them to reach the pole.

'To get our minds off this biting cold, why don't we all say what we'd like best for Christmas,' says Wilson in his cheeriest voice. 'I'll start. For Christmas this year I would like a hot bath followed by a good few hours spent by the fireside with a glass of port.'

'I like the sound of that, Uncle Bill,' says Taff. 'But for one thing. I'd like to add a roasted turkey to your evening by the fire. I've got a funny feeling that back at Cape Evans they'll be having one of Clissold's ghastly seal-meat creations. No, I'll take roast turkey any day. With lots of stuffing. And you can keep your port. I'd much rather have a tankard of ale.'

'If we're working towards a perfect Christmas,' says Scott, 'I'd do just about anything right now to see my boy's face as he opens the Christmas stocking that my dear wife has hung on the end of his bed.'

'Yes indeed, family,' murmurs Wilson. 'Our thoughts are certainly with our families today of all days.'

'And what about you, Oates?' Scott asks, keen to lighten the mood. 'What would you like most of all for Christmas?'

Oates is silent. All he can think of are his feet. Most of all, he wants new feet. Warm feet. Dry feet. Anybody's feet but the two frozen lumps of flesh at the end of his legs.

Scott asks, 'Are you having trouble choosing something, Oates?'

'No sir, I'm not having trouble,' says Oates. He wants to change the subject. He glances back at the action on the crevasse. 'Look, it looks like they've managed to haul Lashly out. We can finally get moving again.'

There's no raging fire that night. Neither is there any ale or port or a hot bath for any of the men celebrating Christmas 1911 on the Antarctic plateau. But there is plenty of good food for the men to enjoy while they discuss the final stage of their polar journey.

'We should be past the worst of the crevasses,' says Scott. 'We'll continue to rise for the next few days. Eventually the land will flatten out. Don't expect spectacular scenery. I'm afraid where we are heading, our days of marching will be rather monotonous. We should all expect colder temperatures too. And fierce winds.'

'At what point will we separate?' asks Oates. 'I mean, when will you send the last group back?'

'I think around New Year. Once we reach 87 degrees south, we'll make one final depot.'

Oates is quietly hopeful of staying on. Being part of Scott's sledging party has been worthwhile. They've pulled well as a team – Wilson, Taff, Scott and himself – and Scott's set a good pace even for an old man of forty-three. Oates can't imagine any of them being sent home early. Scott's not so hateful after all – Oates feels bad for all the captain-bashing he's done in the letters to his mother. He'll make sure to set her straight, make things right when they get back.

'Good hoosh,' says Wilson. 'Pemmican, slices of horse-meat, onions, curry powder and plenty of biscuits to soak in it. This is a fine meal indeed.'

'What about the turkey with stuffing?' Taff laughs. 'I was led to believe that we could have anything we wanted for Christmas.' He elbows Wilson in the side. 'Isn't that what you were saying, Doc?'

'I'm afraid I failed to find a turkey wandering the wilds this afternoon, Taff.' Wilson grins. 'Will plum pudding, caramels and ginger do?'

Taff licks his spoon. 'I suppose it will have to – under the present circumstances.'

'And for you, Robert? Plum pudding?' asks Wilson.

Scott shakes his head. 'I am afraid, Bill, that I am defeated.'

CHAPTER FORTY

Crean is crying. 'I'm sorry, sir,' he splutters.

'You've done well, Crean,' Scott pats him on the shoulder. 'You all have.' He looks from Crean to Lashly to Lieutenant Evans. 'We couldn't have got this far without you. And now you get to return home, to see all our friends at Cape Evans before they head away on the *Terra Nova.*'

The three men standing in front of Scott listen to his words but they each find it difficult to see any advantages to heading home this close to the pole. Lashly is dog tired. He'd like to cry but won't allow himself to show how disappointed he really is. Together with Lieutenant Evans, he's

hauled a sledge since the motor sledges gave out – a staggering 643 kilometres further than the other team.

'Birdie,' says Lieutenant Evans. 'Can I give you this to
take with you?'

Bowers looks at the bright silk flag that Evans has
forced into his mitts.

'My wife wanted me to fly it at the pole. I'm sure she
won't mind who places it there – just as long as I can tell her
it made the final journey.'

Bowers smiles. It's an odd thing to be the only one of
his sledging mates to remain with Scott. Evans, Lashly and
Crean will have a long slow pull with only three of them
hauling. Still, the sledges are both much lighter since they
unloaded the excess weight to create Three Degree Depot.
Crean and Taff have made a great job of cutting down the
two three and a half metre sledges into slightly shorter
sledges. It's a tough job to undertake any carpentry without
adequate tools, but in minus-30-degree conditions, the
two men have had to work very quickly to get the job done.
A 3 metre sledge should be easier even over the dreadful
sastrugi that they've found up on the plateau. As the only
one not on skis, Bowers is untroubled by the sastrugi,
powering up and over the frozen waves with his short legs
pumping. They'll all be abandoning their silly planks and
taking to their feet if the surface doesn't improve.

Scott has a bit to tell the returning party. Knowing as he does that he won't be back at Cape Evans before the *Terra Nova* returns and again sets sail, Scott is facing a second winter season at Cape Evans. He's asked Lieutenant Evans to send Meares back out onto the Ice Barrier with his two dog teams towards the middle of February. Scott and the pole party are sure to need support on the return journey and will welcome a chance to load up the dogs with any extra weight.

While Scott and Evans talk, Oates scribbles down a note for his mother: '*I am afraid the letter I wrote from the hut was full of grumbles but I was very anxious about starting off with those ponies. If anything should happen to me on this trip, which I don't think likely, ask for my notebook. I have written instructions on the fly leaf that it is to be sent to you but please remember that when a man is having a hard time he says hard things about other people which he would regret afterwards.*'

He hands the note to Evans. 'For my mother,' Oates says. 'Please make sure this reaches her if the worst should happen.'

Evans nods. As much as he would like to tell his wife that he was among the first men to reach the South Pole, there is also a small part of him that is relieved that the endless hard slog will soon come to an end. He is fearfully tired.

Oates says, 'You won't have much of a slope going back, but old Christopher is waiting to be eaten on the Barrier when you get there.'

Everybody laughs. It seems so long ago that the world's most troublesome pony raced around their campsite, trying to escape Oates and the rifle he had aimed at the creature's head. Having hauled the sledges themselves for a month, the men have a renewed appreciation for what the ponies accomplished.

The sun is shining when the men farewell their travelling companions. One party heads north, the other south. With the sun at their backs, Scott and his four men know that at noon, their shadows will be pointing them in the right direction. Lashly, Crean and Lieutenant Evans raise three cheers and watch as five of the luckiest men alive head onwards towards 90 degrees south.

CHAPTER FORTY-ONE

The hand is throbbing in the reindeer mitt but at least the bleeding has stopped. Taff curses himself for being so careless. If he had been more focused on his tools, he wouldn't be in this mess. But his hands were so hopeless in his mitts; he'd never have managed the modifications to the two sledges if he hadn't taken them off. The cut goes deep. Holding his ski poles is pure agony. But as painful as his injury is, Taff refuses to let anyone know. Instead, he occupies his mind with thoughts of the pub he'll open back in Wales when he returns a famous polar explorer.

The men have now passed 88 degrees south, the point at which Ernest Shackleton gave up and turned for home.

It is a very exciting prospect for them to be setting out across an area of land that no man has set foot on in the entire history of the world. They need all the motivation they can muster. Never have they had such hard pulling. The sledge rasps and creaks, sinking ever deeper in the soft snow. Their load is lighter than ever, and yet they tug and strain in their harnesses to advance at their slowest pace. Scott wonders if it is neither the snow conditions nor their sledge. Perhaps they are simply becoming weaker. For two weeks they've been pulling in high altitude where the air is thinner, and the lungs must work hard to draw enough oxygen into the bloodstream. Every movement is an effort. Even with good rations, the constant physical stress is taking its toll on them. Their bodies are slowing wasting away. Their faces are haggard. Their skin, pounded by wind, snow and sun, is dark, puffy and scabbed over in places.

Time is precious. With limited provisions and fuel for cooking and melting snow, they must make up the distance or face turning around like Shackleton, a mere 80 kilometres from their goal.

The sky is overcast. The men walk into the white. Nothingness lies before them. Only a rational mind would believe they were still on earth. They're all feeling colder than usual, even though the temperature is comparatively mild. The fur covering has rubbed off their finnesko boots after so many hundreds of kilometres of hard slog, and their feet feel exposed, with only several layers of woollen socks for insulation. Scott has taken to slathering his feet with grease in the evenings – a difficult task now that there are five men in the four-man tent. Oates continues to suffer in silence. He's beginning to feel rather homesick.

They pull over the razor backs of the sastrugi, the sledge bumping up and down, jerking them back whenever they cannot clear the humps in one go. They all feel that they must be getting close, and with no sign of Amundsen's party or tracks in the snow, they allow themselves to hope that victory is within reach.

On 16 January, Bowers's careful measurements tell them that they are within a day's march of the pole. By his reckoning, there are only 12 kilometres remaining. Spirits are high. The men chat excitedly over lunch about finally getting to the only point on the globe where all directions point north. It is a queer thought.

'Robert, Taff has just shown me his hand,' says Wilson as the others begin to pack up for the afternoon march. 'It seems he hurt it a while ago when he and Crean were modifying the sledges.'

'Why didn't you say anything, man?'

Taff shrugs. 'Didn't seem important.'

Wilson continues. 'The hand is badly infected and

oozing fluid. I've drained the pus and dressed the wound properly. It should be fine now.'

Scott is disappointed it wasn't picked up earlier. 'Taff, did you think I'd have sent you home with the others?'

Taff nods. 'The thought did cross my mind.'

'Well, you needn't have worried. You are a giant worker, Taff. We owe such a lot to you. Our ski shoes and crampons have been absolutely indispensable . . . and now seeing how you take responsibility for every sledge, tent, sleeping bag and harness, and thinking out and arranging the packing of the sledge – you're for keeps.'

It's nice to be reassured. But overhearing their conversation doesn't change Oates's mind – he's still not about to reveal to his companions that his feet are not showing any signs of improving.

Bowers's navigation skills are excellent. And so is his eyesight. He's the first one to see the disturbance on the horizon. He's not sure what it is. He doesn't want to say what he thinks it could be. He struggles on in silence for a few minutes. Finally he can't keep his thoughts to himself.

'I can see something.'

'What is it?' asks Scott.

'I'm not sure,' Bowers feels a hot burst in the pit of his stomach. 'But it looks like a cairn. Then again, it might just be a particularly tall run of sastrugi.'

Nobody says anything more. They walk. They think. They hope against hope that what Bowers sees on the horizon is a mirage, a trick of the light.

But there can be no mistake. And, uttering the words, Bowers sinks all their dreams. 'It's a flag, Captain. It's a black flag.'

CHAPTER FORTY-TWO

Scott peers into the abandoned tent. Once again he scans the letter left for him among the Norwegians' discarded belongings.

> *Dear Captain Scott,*
>
> *As you are probably the first to reach this area after us, I will ask you kindly to forward this letter to King Haakon VII. If you can use any of the articles left in the tent please do not hesitate to do so. With kind regards. I wish you a safe return.*
>
> *Yours truly*
>
> *Roald Amundsen*

'If nobody wants these,' says Bowers, holding up a pair of mitts, 'I could use them.'

Nobody objects. In fact, nobody says a thing. There are no words to describe the sense of loneliness they each feel when confronting the awful truth. More than two and a half months after leaving Cape Evans, they have triumphed in reaching their goal, only to have failed in their quest to be first.

'Thirty-four days,' says Wilson. 'That's all that separates us from them.'

'Don't forget, they had a 100 kilometre head start coming from the Bay of Whales. One hundred kilometres closer to the pole than we were at Cape Evans.' Oates says wearily, knowing that none of it matters now.

'So Amundsen found an easier way up,' says Scott. 'That is what we must assume.'

Bowers stands up straight. 'We've got here and, if ever a journey has been accomplished by honest sweat, ours has.'

'Indeed,' says Scott. 'It is something to have got here.'

Nobody can argue with the sentiment. Despite a strong icy headwind and aching hands and feet, they press on for a few more kilometres to the precise location of the South Pole. Having discussed among themselves if it is worth the effort, they all agree that they must make sure the Norwegians have not failed on a technicality. Sure enough, the spot is accurately marked. Without delay, Scott and his men erect a cairn from blocks of snow, attach the Union Jack to a ski pole and take a series of photos. Nobody smiles. This is not a happy day.

Scott's thoughts turn north. He must rally his men if they are to make it back to Cape Evans before winter. From now on, a hasty retreat is their one and only concern.

'Right!' he says, slipping back into leadership mode. 'It is time to draw a curtain of mercy on our ambition and face the 1200 kilometre homeward stretch. Let's say goodbye to our daydreams and focus on safety and speed. At least the wind will be at our backs.'

Great dark snow clouds are gathering. They block out the sun and shower the five men with a fine haze of ice crystals, the sort that make the business of hauling a trial. Their old tracks are soon obscured, making it desperately difficult to navigate back to the site where they made their final depot. The cold wind bites at their heels. The colder it becomes, the faster they'll need to haul to keep their blood pumping to their extremities. They cannot pause.

Scott's heart is breaking. 'Great God,' he says to himself. 'This is an awful place.'

CHAPTER FORTY-THREE

Oates stares at his toe. Purple is such an unnatural colour for skin. It's not painful. The blackening toe doesn't even feel like it belongs to his body. It sits on the end of his foot like a strange insect. But pulling on his socks over the blistered skin of his frostbitten feet is an ordeal that sends him into paroxysms of blinding pain that he finds hard to mask. Ten days march from the pole and the pressure from his finnesko boots is close to unbearable.

Taff is also suffering. His hands are a mess of red and yellow blisters. The damaged nerve endings of his fingertips sparkle with pain. Frequent frostbites have given his nose the appearance of a terrible vegetable, raw and misshapen.

Wilson lies with his eyes closed. The zinc sulfate drops do little for the incessant burn behind his eyelids. He won't sleep well, if at all, this night. Marching north into the glare of the sun has been pure torture. Keeping a visual record of the expedition has meant spending extended periods of time with no eye protection. After sketching Amundsen's flag at the pole, Wilson has largely given it up. Even during the evenings in the tent, his hands are too cold to hold his pencil firmly.

'We're making fine progress,' says Scott. 'Another day of 26 kilometres.'

The men murmur approval. Too tired to make much conversation, they prefer to sit in companionable silence and enjoy the brief rest. None of them feels they ever get enough sleep. All of them are hungry.

'Against all odds, we've managed to find the supply depots so far. I think this system of fanning out whenever we lose sight of our old tracks is working for us. And Bowers, I congratulate you on your expert handling of the theodolite. Using the sun's position at noon to work out our latitude takes extreme patience. I know this wind makes it the coldest work possible and I thank you for your diligence.'

'Yes, well done,' says Wilson.

'Indeed,' murmurs Oates without a great deal of enthusiasm.

Taff can't muster a response. He's fallen asleep.

Scott doesn't like how the weather is breaking up. It's getting late in the season and he's desperate to get off the summit before winter arrives. Already they've suffered through a week of blizzard conditions, and the tent and equipment are badly iced up. The sleeping bags are getting wetter and heavier. The gale is still howling outside. It gave them a terrible time when they were trying to get the tent up. Double layers of flapping canvas, whipping them in the face. Oates and Taff can't take the wind much anymore. They're both so prone to frostbite.

The blizzards are punishing, waylaying progress and dumping more sandy snow in their path. They must press on. They have enough food as long as they can find the depots they laid on the way to the pole. On the outward journey they made cairns at both lunch and evening camps, but in white-out conditions, when all definition is lost, spotting them is close to impossible.

The following morning Scott rouses the men earlier than usual. But it takes them even longer to break camp. Once such a tireless worker, Taff finds any folding, strapping or fastening of the loads excruciating work for his hands. By far the biggest and most muscular of the men on setting out from Cape Evans, Taff is now the thinnest.

The featureless landscape of the summit plateau greets them, rolling on and on to the horizon in every direction. On the count of three, the men hoist their sail – the floor cloth from the tent, which they've attached to ski poles. The sledge won't glide off on its own and it certainly won't carry the weary party home, but harnessing the power of the wind will share some of the physical burden of hauling. The mental burden is still theirs to bear alone.

Wilson has strained a tendon in his leg. Badly swollen, the limb needs rest above all, but they can't afford to lose a day. Instead, Wilson will walk beside the sledge while the four remaining manhaulers heave and sweat and curse under their breath. Wilson finds the day one of the hardest yet. Not because of the pain he's in, but because of being so useless. Even Taff with his ravaged hands can still pull. He lost two fingernails in the night. Wilson dressed the oozing wounds the best he could. Taff held his breath when Wilson bent down and sniffed at the raw flesh. It is a relief that, as yet, there is no sign of gangrene.

CHAPTER FORTY-FOUR

'We've made it!' Bowers shouts.

'Land ahoy,' breathes Captain Scott.

It is no mirage dancing on the horizon. It really is rock – black rock. The mountains flanking the Beardmore are distant and splendid. Relief overcomes them like a warm wave. They'll soon be upon the upper glacier depot.

'I never thought I'd be so thrilled to see the Beardmore Glacier again,' says Wilson. 'A heavenly sight indeed.'

Oates smiles broadly, his waxy yellow cheeks stretching painfully. 'It does me a world of good even looking at it,' he says. 'Finally, something other than whiteness to walk towards. Wouldn't you say, Taff?'

Taff grunts. If he's smiling nobody can see under the shaggy beard that covers the lower half of his face. If only he could grow a beard for protection over his poor damaged nose. It looks as though it has started to rot. The Welshman could use some good news. He hasn't been his old cheerful self for weeks.

It's early February. The most dangerous stage of the return journey lies before them. Picking a way down the treacherous and ever-changing ice falls will test their navigation abilities as well as their survival skills.

Their strategy of following old tracks has not been without problems. The constant weaving around pressure ridges on the outward journey has made following them on the way home a long and frustrating task. Even after reaching the spot where Lieutenant Evans and the others turned back, with its three distinct tracks to follow, the going has been tough. Ultimately, they've decided to leave the tracks and instead concentrate on heading due north.

Wilson says, 'I hope to have an opportunity to collect those samples of rock I promised Wright.' He's pulling again. Either his leg is no longer bothering him or he can no longer bear watching the others do all the work. He knows Taff is flagging and Oates is exhausted. He must do his part – it may not be best for him, but it's best for the team.

Bowers is as full of bustle and energy as usual. Never a complaint crosses his lips although, like the others, he's famished. Lunch is worst. They're on full rations but it never seems to satisfy. He thinks of the pony meat they'll be able to get into when they make it back down to the depots on the Barrier. How he'll sink his teeth into the chewy meat. If only he could eat it twice.

The land doesn't seem to get any closer over the course of the day. The way forward is becoming ever more problematic, with pressure ridges rising to block their passage every few hours. Scott leads the team west for a time, then, turning back northward, discovers a colossal crevasse, yawning wide and horribly deep. They can see land, but how do they reach it?

The sky becomes overcast. Entering a crevasse-riddled zone, the conditions are far from ideal. Food is getting low and the weather is uncertain. They must arrive at their upper glacier depot soon. All this backtracking does little for morale, Scott thinks to himself. And keeping up morale is critical.

Suddenly Scott slips. He's down. His harness arrests his fall. To his left is Taff, also hanging by his harness. Taff cradles the back of his head. He's already fallen down a crevasse today. Scott feels the harness tighten across his chest as the three men on the surface drag their leader to safety. When Taff appears, he's still rubbing his head. He's taken a heavy knock.

'Are you alright, Taff?' Scott says.

Taff doesn't speak.

'Taff,' Scott says again. 'Are you alright?'

The men gather to Taff's side. He seems disorientated. He looks at them for a moment, blinking, as if trying to gather his thoughts. 'Gee,' he manages finally. 'I took a bit of a tumble.'

Bowers pats him on the back. 'Shall we carry on?'

Blank faced, Taff stares at Bowers.

Wilson peers into his eyes. 'Shall we rest?'

Taff is silent. He rubs his head again.

'Do you need a rest?' Scott asks more forcefully. 'Do we need to set up camp?'

'No. No,' says Taff abruptly. 'We can go on.'

Scott pauses, looks at Wilson. It's not a good place to camp but he's keen for Wilson's medical opinion.

Wilson shrugs his shoulders. 'If he says to carry on, then we should carry on.'

CHAPTER FORTY-FIVE

Scott is pleased to have the sun on his face. To be standing on firm rock after forty-eight days of trudging on the snow and ice of the summit plateau feels like stepping ashore after months at sea. It's warmer on the glacier too, and pleasantly free of wind, sheltered as they are under the towering sandstone cliffs shot through with seams of coal. Scott has called a halt for the afternoon so Wilson can gather rock samples. Oates and Taff are resting in the tent. Bowers, as restless and busy as always, has cast off in search of more interesting geological finds. Scott stares in wonder at the rock in his hand. Fossilised leaves. Amazing. So clear. So visible after

250 million years. How astonishing to think of the dense foliage spilling over, covering every surface of this lifeless landscape.

Scott shifts his gaze north. It will be more difficult picking a path down the glacier than it was on the way up, when everything was laid out in plain view. Navigating through the ice field without a map, with no way of rising above it and seeing the lay of the land, is a daunting prospect. But having done it once before, Scott is sure to manage it again.

Three days later, Scott is no longer so sure his navigation skills can be relied upon.

'We're lost again, aren't we?' Oates says, frustrated.

'Lost is the wrong word,' says Scott. 'That implies we're following a known route. I'm afraid we have no route to follow. This is a process of discovery.'

'We'll have to discover ourselves out of this dead end then, won't we?' Oates fumes. He's sick of following. Scott's wild guesses have proved wildly wrong at every turn. For six hours they've been going round in circles, doubling back and creeping forward at a snail's pace. The mist is lowering and with only three days' worth of rations remaining, this madness can't continue.

'Shall we head back east, see if things open up a bit for us there? We haven't tried that yet,' suggests Bowers.

Wilson is losing patience too, with so much uncertainty. He's fed up with stopping. Since removing their skis, not a minute goes by without someone needing to free a foot from a crevasse. 'Bowers, listen, if there'd been a clear way out we'd have seen it from the ridge. We have to stick to the left. I know it will be further but as far as I see it, it's our best shot of clearing this turmoil.'

Scott listens to the bickering with a heavy heart. He can't help feeling that the mess is his fault. Navigating is his responsibility but he's as confused as anyone.

Another six hours pass with little progress northward. But at least with the wind picking up, the mist is clearing, giving them a more complete picture of their situation. It is 10pm. They make camp, hopeful that a hot meal and some sleep will improve their outlook. With no idea of how much longer they will need to battle on to reach the next depot, a decision is made to stretch their three-day ration to four days. Hunger is only one of their problems.

Another day of turmoil follows. Their situation becomes critical. The petty fights continue, each man offering a different opinion on which direction is best. When they stumble into a maze of crevasses, they give in to fatigue, make their camp and consume their second-to-last meal ration.

Scott does not sleep well. He's up in the night, forever scanning the sky for signs of bad weather. It closes in shortly before dawn and by 8am the snow is falling thick around them. They could stay in their sleeping bags but everybody is anxious to continue. The thought of no food is the only motivation they need to set out afresh. The surroundings are hazardous in the extreme. After an hour of pathfinding through broken ice, the men step out onto a gravel strewn track. Suddenly pulling becomes easier, the light improves. The sky peels back its dull shroud.

'The depot!' Taff yells. It's the loudest noise he's made in a long while. 'I can see the depot.'

'Where?' asks Scott, attempting to follow Taff's line of sight.

'Look, over there. Below that dark patch of rock.'

Bowers is craning his neck. 'Can't be,' he says. 'All the way over there?'

They're all excited but none of them can make out clearly what Taff is talking about. Drawing nearer, it becomes obvious that what he thought was the depot is nothing but an odd-shaped shadow on the ice.

'I can't believe it,' says Oates. 'After all of that. All my hopes . . .'

'Don't kiss them goodbye just yet,' says Wilson, pointing off into the distance. 'If I'm not mistaken myself, there is a red flag flapping over there in the distance.'

'Food, glorious food,' coos Bowers. 'I'm going to carve

216

myself off a great big slice of roast pork and crackling and wolf it down with a plate of creamy mashed potato.'

Oates says, 'I'm going to bite into a steaming hot Cornish pasty – with peas and carrots, smothered in brown sauce.'

'Steak and onions for me,' says Wilson.

'Just a tankard of ale for me,' grunts Taff.

'So does that mean I can polish off all the pemmican myself?' Scott asks.

It's the first joke they've shared in a long while. It may well be their last.

CHAPTER FORTY-SIX

Taff's acting oddly. It's the third time he's stopped the march.

'Birdie?'

'Yes, Taff?'

'Can I borrow some string?'

'Some string? Why on earth do you need string?' asks Bowers.

'We don't have any string!' shouts Oates. 'We're in the middle of Antarctica.'

'Taff, we can't keep stopping like this.' Scott knows Taff is exhausted, he knows Taff is nursing the largest blister he's ever seen on the sole of his right foot. But Scott's patience is wearing thin.

Oates can't contain his anger. 'You're behaving worse than an old woman. Pull yourself together.'

Wilson gives Scott an anxious look. 'Perhaps Taff can take a break from pulling, Robert. I fear his crampons are cutting into his feet in the worst possible way.'

'He's not the only one,' Oates mutters. 'We're all suffering.'

Food is running short again. They must reach the lower glacier depot in the next day. Scott has already spoken anxiously about the delays in breaking camp with Taff, who is no longer capable of lending any help at all. If they're to cover the required distance between depots, they must have the hours to do it. Leaving camp an hour late is an hour they cannot make up on the march. They must get on.

Wilson wants nothing less in the world than to stall for longer in the cold, but he says, 'Taff, come over here and I'll try to adjust your crampons for you.'

Bowers leans close to Scott. 'He's absolutely changed. He's a different person. There's no sign of the old Taff – the big strong ox of a man who'd do anything for anyone at any time of the day or night.'

'Worse than an old woman,' Oates says again under his breath.

'There is no doubt. He's broken down in the brain.' Scott is seriously worried. This could be the end of all of them. The weather is against them, they're hungry, freezing cold and short of rest. They cannot afford to fall behind with a sick man. 'Taff can walk beside the sledge,' he calls out to Wilson. 'Can you manage that, Taff?'

Taff nods as he gets to his feet.

It's a terrible day. The land is hazy, the snow is soft and sticky and clings to the sledge runners as the four man-haulers drag their infernal dead weight onward. Taff plods heavily beside the sledge, stopping from time to time to stare at his surroundings. After an hour, there's a distance of twenty metres between him and the sledge. The men wait for Taff to catch up, then give a series of forceful pulls to get their solid load moving once more.

'Taff, you mustn't fall behind. I realise it's hard going for you now, but you must follow on quickly. Not only could you lose sight of us but we can't afford to wait for you in this cold. We need to keep moving and so do you.' Scott delivers his sternest warning yet.

'Yes sir, I will,' Taff nods vigorously. But before long, he has fallen even further behind. Reluctant to halt again, the men continue hauling, glancing back every now and then to check that the Welshman is still moving in the right direction, however slowly.

Bowers speaks first. 'He's fallen fearfully behind.'

Scott turns back. 'Good heavens, he has. We'll have to halt our march.'

'Perhaps we should stop for lunch,' says Wilson. 'Warm up a little. We have a slow road ahead of us, I fear.'

'Good idea,' says Scott. 'Let's move swiftly. Get the tent up. Taff should see it quite clearly. We'll be able to get a hot meal into him by the time he gets here.'

Sure enough, the hoosh is ready, the tea is finished. The men talk of what lies ahead. Still no sign of Taff. The men eat. They talk some more. Still no Taff.

'We'll have to go and look for him,' Scott's anxiety is clear to everyone in the tent.

The four men fan out, back along the tracks they've left in the snow before lunch. Several hundred metres on, they see him.

'Taff! What have you done?' Wilson kneels beside Taff in the snow. 'Your gloves? Where are they?'

'Good God!' Scott cries. 'Get his clothes back on.'

Taff has a wild look in his eyes. Oates and Bowers work frantically. Taff's clothes are in total disarray. He seems to have got tangled in his harness, his wind blouse is off and dragging in the snow. Scott whips off his mitts and hands them to Wilson. Taff's mottled hands are buried deep in the snow. But for the bloody bandages, they're completely bare.

221

Once the mitts are on, Scott and Wilson lift Taff to his feet. He's thin but he's still a big man and difficult to manage between the two of them.

'Let's get you walking, Taff,' Wilson encourages. 'Let's warm you up.'

Taff manages a few steps then falls to his knees, crumpling once again onto the snow. Oates and Bowers look on, powerless.

'We need the sledge,' says Scott with a nervous tone seldom heard in his voice. 'Oates, you stay here.'

Bowers, Wilson and Scott charge back to camp. Oates sits with Taff, holding his hand and talking about anything he can think of.

'How about that pub of yours Taff, in Swansea. It's bound to be a great success, I know it. I'll come and visit you there. I'll sit at the bar and order a drink from my old pal Taff. If you're lucky I'll order another round and another and another. Before long, I'll be drunk and you'll be rich.'

Taff murmurs.

Oates peers off through the haze for any sign of the others returning.

'We'll get you back to the tent. Feed you up. We'll get you back into your sleeping bag and you'll have a nice warm nap. When you wake up you'll feel right as rain again. No harm done. No harm, Taff. Everything's going to be fine.

And before you know it, we'll be back on the Barrier and heading home to Cape Evans where I just know Clissold will be warming a plate of seal's liver just for you.'

Taff murmurs again. He might be laughing. It might be a groan of pain. Oates can't be sure.

'Here they are, Taff. I can see them. They've got the sledge. We'll have you on it in no time.'

Taff is unconscious by the time they return to the tent. No hot meal will pass his lips. Bowers and Wilson slip his frigid body into its sleeping bag. They all watch. And wait. The end comes just after midnight. Wilson says a prayer. Scott records Taff's death in his diary as 17 February.

With no spade to dig a grave and too cold to linger, the four men leave Taff's body on the glacier, confident that what they themselves cannot do for their friend, nature will soon accomplish.

CHAPTER FORTY-SEVEN

It may have been christened 'Shambles Camp' on the outward journey, but the four remaining men find nothing out of order in the depot at the base of the Beardmore Glacier. As the final resting place of the expedition's hardest working ponies, Shambles Camp offers up a feast of pony meat. The frozen flesh is much needed. The men are wasting away eating food that doesn't provide the necessary calories or nutrients for their bodies to carry on as they have over many months.

The worst of their journey is behind them. They have Taff's rations for extra sustenance. There's just over

640 kilometres to Cape Evans, and 386 kilometres to One Ton Depot. Three depots lie between. A pace of 14 kilometres a day will see them through. They should be fine. But having struggled over the rotten Barrier surface once before, the men know the final stage of their journey home will be far from easy.

Taff is still in their thoughts. Nobody feels good. Leaving his body exposed to the elements like that, even when it was vital to their own survival to move on. And now to be four in the tent again. While the extra room makes things a little more comfortable, the men still huddle together in their sleeping bags when it's time to turn in.

A long, eight-hour sleep means they're late getting organised. Scott sees no need to hurry the others. They swap their old sledge for one of the sledges that was left at the camp. They need to make some adjustments to fit their mast and packing the precious pony meat takes time. When they finally draw out of Shambles Camp, it's past noon. The sun is shining and there is not a breath of wind. They could use a southerly – anything to fill their sail and get them through the deep snow. It is like hauling a dead elephant over desert sands. Perhaps the problem is that they are sheltered by the mountains. Once they move further out on the Barrier, there is sure to be a strong wind to harden the surface and give them a good push from behind.

It's terribly slow progress to Desolation Camp – where the blizzard waylaid them for four days on the journey south. They see the snow walls, erected to lend shelter to the poor ponies during the storm. So much depends on the weather. Even out here, beyond the shadow of the mountains, there's still no wind. The sledge drags, acting like a horrible brake on their exertions. A paltry 10-kilometre march is all they can show for a full day of hard slog. Clearly they're not as fit as they used to be. And they are all so desperately cold. The temperatures are lower than expected. Winter is fast approaching.

'I'm going to enjoy seeing Christopher again,' says Oates, as he clears away the snow from the supplies. The men have reached the Southern Barrier Depot on 23 February. Replenishing their food and fuel is a priority.

Bowers laughs. 'That pony won't be giving you any more trouble, will he?'

'Here he is.' It's the pony's mane. Oates gives a tug and the whole of Christopher's head appears from the loose drift.

'Oh. That doesn't look too good,' says Bowers. 'That meat is quite rotten.'

Oates frowns. 'Thankfully no smell. But you're right, Birdie. We won't be eating that.'

'Someone hasn't done their job,' says Bowers sourly,

226

meaning Meares. 'It hasn't been buried properly. The sun's got at it. A shocking waste.' He kicks snow back over the spoiled meat. 'I cannot abide shoddy work.' It's a mistake Bowers himself would never have made.

Oates gets to his feet. He bangs the snow from his mitts. 'Christopher's revenge on us.'

The two men carry the cans of paraffin to load onto the sledge.

'This feels quite empty,' says Bowers. He gives the can a shake. 'There's barely any in there!'

'Come to think of it, this one feels a little light too,' says Oates.

Bowers checks all the cans. One is empty, one is full and two have half left. It's bad, very bad. He must inform the Captain.

'I can't understand it,' says Scott in the tent. 'There don't appear to be any holes in the can. We'd have noticed if it had seeped into the snow. They haven't spilled . . .'

'Evaporation?' says Wilson, stirring the evening pemmican. 'If those cans were in the sun for any length of time, the paraffin vapor could have escaped out the lids even if they were properly screwed on.'

'Yes, but so much of it?' Scott is confused.

'It has been sitting out here for a year,' says Bowers. 'And the leather washers have dried and cracked in the cold.'

'We don't have much oil left then, do we?' Oates knows the answer. They all do.

'We shall have to be very careful,' says Scott. 'We won't be eating cold meals but we can't afford to warm the tent at all or dry our socks out like we have been doing. Not until we get to the next depot, at least. But if the same should have happened to the other oil supplies, I'm not sure what we'll do.'

Bowers says, 'We do have the lamp, with the methylated spirits. Could we use that instead?'

'Good thinking, Birdie. You're right. We could,' Scott smiles. 'I love your resourcefulness. It's why you're on this expedition.'

The men enjoy their hoosh that evening, in the knowledge that a hot meal may become a luxury. They need it more than ever, relying on the heat in their bellies to force warmth back to their frozen fingers and toes. Nothing will dry in the extreme cold of the tent and the prospect of slipping feet into wet or frozen footwear is depressing at best. Oates has the hardest time of all. Wilson has made a deep cut in Oates' finneskos to allow him to get his swollen feet into the boots. How he manages to walk on them is a wonder.

'What of the dogs?' asks Oates.

'Well, I told Meares to bring them out to meet us early to mid-March,' says Scott. 'To the camp at One Ton and beyond to the Mt Hooper depot if possible.'

'What if he chooses to leave on the *Terra Nova*? Wasn't that his plan?' asks Bowers. 'I know he's keen to get back to his family.'

'In that case, I told Evans when he left us on the summit plateau that Atkinson should bring the dogs out to meet us. We could really use the dogs' help with hauling. And with extra rations.'

'Assuming Meares and the dog teams got back alright,' says Wilson, raising his eyebrows.

'Yes,' agrees Scott. 'I did ask him to accompany us part way up the glacier, which is 200 kilometres further than he wanted to come. But he should have got back alright.'

'Well, I for one look forward to seeing those dogs,' says Oates. It's the closest he's come to revealing just how much pain he is in, now that all his toes have turned black.

CHAPTER FORTY-EIGHT

The middle of the Barrier is an achingly empty place. The temperature has plummeted to minus 40 degrees. Everything takes longer in the unimaginable cold. Even a task as simple as easing cold feet into footwear takes an hour. By the time the men break camp, load up and harness themselves to the sledge, the warming effect of their hot breakfast has all but disappeared.

At long last the wind has picked up. But it's coming from the wrong direction to help with the sail. In fact, the freezing wind blows in their faces, making the already heavy hauling close to impossible. The men barely cover

8 kilometres a day. Travelling at such a painfully slow rate, the men get colder and colder on the march. And their fuel situation has not improved.

'Can I show you something, Uncle Bill?' says Oates after the evening meal, a barely warm slurry of pemmican.

Wilson peers over at Oates fumbling with his sock.

'Good Lord!' he exclaims. 'You poor chap.'

Scott stops writing in his diary. Bowers also looks around to see the dreadful sight. The foot appears dead. Swollen to bursting, the toes completely black. Oates's toenails are thickened and yellow.

'I'm sure I could snap them off if I wanted,' laughs Oates. He's more resigned than bitter.

'What about the other foot, Oates?' asks Scott gently.

'The same.'

Bowers can't believe his eyes. 'But you've been marching – just like we all have.'

'I haven't had a choice,' says Oates. 'I'm not one for hitching a lift.'

'No Surrender Oates, that's what they called you in your old regiment, isn't it?' Scott asks. Unable to help Oates in any meaningful way, Scott focuses on cheering him up.

'My old regiment . . .' Oates says. 'I want to make them proud. Keep on as long as I can.'

'Why No Surrender Oates?' asks Bowers.

'Boer War. I was shot in the thigh. Shattered the bone. I wouldn't surrender.' Oates shrugs. 'It's no worse than what I've seen out here.'

Scott says, 'I am sure they would be proud of you, having marched to the South Pole and back. As we do not know if Amundsen has made it safely home, we may find that we are the only men to have reached 90 degrees south and lived to tell the tale.'

'Chance would be a fine thing,' says Oates.

'Let's see what we can do about these feet, shall we?' says Wilson briskly. 'I'm sure we'll get a lot more wear out of them yet.'

The atmosphere in the tent is cheerful. Nobody wants to admit to feeling worried, to having doubts. But looking at Oates's feet, none of them can help but wonder how much further they can travel with him in tow.

CHAPTER FORTY-NINE

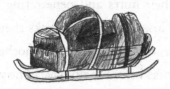

'This uncooked pemmican is really not bad at all,' says Bowers, taking another bite of the solid brown mass.

Wilson murmurs his agreement. 'I actually prefer it this way.'

'As do I,' says Scott. 'It makes a nice change.'

They eat in silence, savouring their lukewarm cups of tea. The evenings are dark now, as winter wraps itself around them.

Oates no longer says much. Wilson has spent a good part of the evening seeing to his feet, dressing them, easing the fluid out of the worst of the blisters and carefully replacing his socks. Gangrene is sure to set in, if it hasn't already. The smell of rotting flesh is a hard odour to mask – none of them will fail to notice when his flesh finally starts to rot on his bones.

Pulling over high mounds of sastrugi all day has left the men too depleted for conversation. The sledge capsized twice during the march. More precious time lost. The wind piercing their mitts and penetrating their clothing. Frequently they lose sight of the tracks they are following. Fanning out, they can usually pick up another sign of where the sledging parties before them have gone while Oates sits on the sledge, saving his dwindling reserves of energy.

Wilson too winces as he slips his feet into his sleeping bag.

'Sore?' Scott asks. He's sure Wilson is in pain. He's seen the limp. 'You need to take yourself in hand, Bill.'

'I'm fine,' smiles Wilson. 'Really.'

Oates stirs. 'Uncle Bill?'

'Yes,' says Wilson brightly.

'Do I have a chance?'

It takes a while for Wilson to respond. Scott and Bowers hold their breath in the silence. Finally Wilson says, 'I don't know, Titus.'

It's a truthful answer. As dismal as it sounds, it's better than saying 'no'.

CHAPTER FIFTY

Meares is not coming with the dogs. Meares is on board the *Terra Nova*, heading for New Zealand. He hasn't resupplied One Ton Depot, either, as he was instructed to. If the depot was resupplied with enough extra dog food, the dog team could travel further across the Barrier should Scott and his men need assistance. Scott knows Meares wanted to leave. But Atkinson has not been able to replace him as per Scott's later order conveyed by Lieutenant Evans.

The truth is, Lieutenant Evans is very near death. Struck down with scurvy on his return journey from the summit plateau, Evans has only just made it back alive due to the efforts of Crean and Lashly, who pulled him for six days on the back of the sledge. With Wilson away with Scott, Atkinson is the only doctor left at Cape Evans and the only person who has a chance of saving Evans. He must stay with the second-in-command, even if it means disobeying Scott's order. In any case, nobody knows that Scott needs help so desperately.

Instead, it is Cherry-Garrard and Dimitri who set out for One Ton Depot on 25 February. Cherry has never driven one dog, let alone a whole team of them. He has no experience navigating, either. His glasses fog up in the low temperatures. Cherry continues blindly in Dimitri's tracks, nervous about their chances of arriving in the right spot, more than 200 kilometres into the interior of the Great Ice Barrier, with no landmarks to help point the way.

Atkinson has told him to take twenty-four days' food for himself and Dimitri, as well as twenty-one days' food for the two dog teams. Of course, they'll need extra rations for the returning polar party. If there is no sign of Scott, Cherry is to leave supplies at the depot and decide for himself whether he should continue or not. One thing is non-negotiable, and that is that no harm must come to the dogs. Scott has always held firm on this. If he has failed to reach the pole this time around, and it is still unclaimed, Scott intends to make a second attempt the following spring. He will need every single dog alive to accompany the mules that have just been dropped off by the *Terra Nova* to replace the ponies.

It takes Cherry and Dimitri a week to reach One Ton. There is still no sign of Scott and the others after another six days of waiting. But Cherry is not worried. He assumes that Scott would have plenty of food and fuel left. Instead, he is concerned about Dimitri. The Russian dog handler is feeling the cold and the whole right side of his body has gone numb. The dogs are as unpredictable and aggressive as ever, and Cherry is terrified of losing Dimitri and having to handle the wild creatures on his own. Already Cherry is doing most of the work around their camp due to Dimitri's mystery illness. Knowing that he doesn't have the necessary provisions or experience to travel further across the Barrier, he opts for turning back. It is 10 March. It is a decision he will struggle with for the rest of his life.

CHAPTER FIFTY-ONE

The sledge weighs a ton. The tent is encased in sheets of ice and is by far the heaviest item they carry. But they cannot dump it or any of the other equipment. Apart from Wilson's precious rock samples, everything they haul on their sledge is crucial for survival.

Oates has become a hindrance. Although he cannot help it, he leaves everybody waiting in the extreme cold in the morning and at lunch. Wilson is suffering. He is so cold at the end of their latest march that he cannot bend down to unstrap his skis. The oil situation has become dire. With significant shortages at every depot they've reached, the men will soon run out of fuel completely, leaving no way of even obtaining water. Reduced to melting snow in their mouths, the men are chilled from the inside out as well as the outside in. Unpleasant as it is, they must keep hydrated. They must endure their icy mouthfuls.

'What should I do?' asks Oates.

The others look at him blankly.

'You cannot carry on with me like this. I'm a liability. I'll be the death of you all. You have to leave me.'

Scott says, 'We will do nothing of the sort.'

'No way,' says Bowers. 'Impossible.'

'Leave me in my sleeping bag,' says Oates more forcefully. 'You won't have to see me die.'

Scott sighs. The suggestion is the only thing that makes sense. But even if it were to help his own chances of survival, Scott cannot bear the thought of leaving a man alone, alive and defenceless in the snow to perish. 'We cannot do that,' he says again more firmly, as if it's himself he must convince. 'We'll find a way.'

Wilson says, 'We're all bad, Oates. But we must keep on. All of us. Even you. You cannot give up.'

Very little is said in the tent in the evenings. Even Bowers, ever cheerful, ever optimistic, can find few opportunities to say anything positive about their predicament. Scott has been writing in his diary. It is a painful business since working with a pencil requires him to take off his gloves. Every now and then he stops to shake some life into his numb fingers. While the others gave up their own diaries some time ago, Scott, as expedition leader, feels a responsibility to keep a record of their days, however doubtful their prospects. And their prospects are blacker than ever. Scott has just calculated the distance to One Ton Depot and their reserves of food. Even if they manage to cover 9.5 kilometres a day, they will still fall short of One Ton by 19 kilometres when their food and fuel runs out. Dread spreads in the pit of his stomach.

'Wilson, what of your medicine chest? Don't you have the wherewithal for each man to decide the time of his passing?' Scott has been considering this question for some time, but has never breathed a word of it. Now the time is right.

'You are referring to the morphine and the opium tablets?'

'I am,' says Scott.

'I cannot allow it. Suicide is not an option.'

'In your opinion,' says Scott.

'Only God can decide when a man must move on from this world,' says Wilson wearily.

'That may be so, but I would feel better if each of us had the option to examine his own conscience. If things are to get much worse and we are to die like dogs, then the prospect of a quick death is one I should like to consider myself. I think you should hand your supplies over.'

Wilson meets Scott's eyes. 'No.'

Bowers, whose Christian beliefs are as strong as Wilson's, has been quiet until now. 'In principle I agree with you, Wilson, but in practice, I must stand with Scott. We each need an escape if all hope is lost.'

'As for me,' Oates clears his throat, 'I am the only one who is staring death in the face and I say we should have the right to decide the hour and manner of our passing.'

Wilson does not comment.

As glad as he is to have the support of Oates and Bowers, Scott finds no pleasure in outnumbering his friend. Wilson, the man he most admires in the world. 'Either you hand them over, or we ransack the medicine chest.'

Wilson knows he's lost the argument. Reluctantly, he reaches for the medical supplies. There are thirty opium tablets and one tube of morphine. He counts out the tablets – ten for Scott, ten for Bowers and ten for Oates. The morphine he will keep for himself.

Scott slips the tablets into the pocket of Oates' trousers. If he is to take them, he'll need somebody to help retrieve them; his frostbitten hands are as good as useless.

'Make sure my mother gets my diary, Wilson,' Oates says. 'She was the only woman I ever loved.'

CHAPTER FIFTY-TWO

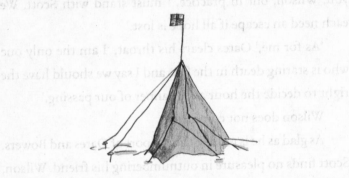

'Is it Friday or Saturday?' Scott writes in his diary. It's not a good question for the leader of a polar expedition to ask himself. But the truth is, Scott is past caring about the day of the week. His world is the blizzard outside the tent. They cannot go on in this. To try is pointless.

Oates has gone.

Nobody says much. They all know that he is walking to his death. His last words ring in their ears: 'I am just going outside and may be some time.'

CHAPTER FIFTY-THREE

Oates had hoped he would not wake up. It would have been easier that way. But now that he is outside the tent, the gale filling his head with its din, he realises that to die like this, bravely facing the whirling white devil, is worthier. His suffering has been intense; hiding it from the others for so long a dreadful challenge. To walk away from the tent, from the torment of burdening his companions, from the unbearable prospect of more days locked in his wretched body, feels liberating. Oates smiles to himself as he strays further and further from his troubles, no longer fighting the probing tentacles of cold as they bury themselves ever deeper. He never guessed that the pain would leave him, as it has now. That he would hear his mother's voice in the wind.

CHAPTER FIFTY-FOUR

Scott, Wilson and Bowers give it two hours. The improvement in the weather is only slight, but it's enough to move on. They pack their equipment. They harness themselves to the sledge. Together they head out into the brutal wind. Oates's sleeping bag, a camera and a theodolite are neatly stacked beside a cairn. In minus 40 degrees the men cannot haul for long. After progressing a few kilometres, they halt their meagre advance, but not before Scott has lost all feeling in his right foot.

'I'm so furious with myself,' he says aloud. 'My foot is gone.'

Bowers asks, 'What do you mean gone? I can see it with my own eyes – on the end of your leg.'

Scott appreciates Birdie's cheerfulness, his attempts at jokes. Wilson is the same – putting on a brave face when everything so clearly suggests disaster. Despite the careful rationing of their fuel, there remains barely half a fill in their primus. A speck of methylated spirits. Perhaps they'll manage a hot cocoa. Maybe another one tomorrow before they set out – nothing more. Their thirst is unbearable, a looming presence that stalks them on their march and lurks in the tent – refusing to go away. How often in their lives have they gulped back clean clear mouthfuls of water without ever appreciating the sweet, satisfying sensation of it running freely down their throats?

'My feet are misbehaving too,' says Wilson. 'I'd gladly leave them behind. Anyone have a spare pair I could borrow? Maybe some kind soul will have stashed a couple of brand-new feet at the depot. Wouldn't that take the cake.'

'Actually, I'll take the cake, not the feet,' Bowers sighs. 'I hope it's chocolate.'

Wilson looks at Scott. He's worried about his friend; he's lost something behind the eyes. His resolve, his energy. This journey has been crushing in every sense of the word. 'We'll get on, Robert. Just you wait. Once you get a hot meal in you again, that foot will recover.'

'Bill,' says Scott, calling Wilson's bluff. 'We both know amputation is the only remedy. These toes . . . they're spoiling.'

'We're barely 18 kilometres from One Ton,' says Bowers. 'What do you say Wilson and I make a break for it? We'll load the fuel and some food onto the empty sledge and hurry back here while you rest up.'

Wilson says, 'I'm in.'

Scott thinks a while. 'Bill, your feet are almost as bad as mine.'

'If we're only pulling a light load, there's little to worry about. We can travel at a faster pace, keep warm. And if we've got a hot meal to look forward to when all is said and done, then that's sure to spur us on, won't it Birdie?' Wilson chuckles. His cracked lips pull tight.

'Just like the Cape Crozier days,' smiles Bowers.

With the howling wind, bitter cold and a poor state of health counting against them, the plan is little more than a suicide mission. Besides, it's not an 18-kilometre journey but a 36-kilometre journey to get there and back. And it will be dark for a significant portion of the time they're gone. They may get lost. They may simply fall over from exhaustion and not be able to get to their feet again. Bowers pushes all the thoughts of failure away. 'Let's take our sleeping bags at least. In case we need to get out of the wind. We've done it before, haven't we, Uncle Bill?'

'Indeed we have. Tried and survived.' Wilson wants to cry.

Scott doesn't have the energy to object. Mostly he admires the pluck and courage of these two men. They're the finest fellows he's had the pleasure of knowing. It is their last chance to turn their situation around.

Having made the decision, the three remaining members of the polar party enjoy their cold pemmican and biscuits and allow the last warm mouthfuls of cocoa to seep into their tired bodies. They sleep well. Better than they have for a long while. But when morning comes, the weather has closed in completely. To venture out would be to admit defeat. And at least two of the men still hold hopes of pulling through. The other is writing letters.

CHAPTER FIFTY-FIVE

The blizzard swarms about the tent. Engulfs it. They cannot leave. The profound cold of winter has them in its death grip. It will not let go. It squeezes itself into sleeping bags, between layers of clothing, and holds fast to bare skin, sucking deeper until it presses against organs and bone.

After a week of no food and only mouthfuls of snow to ease their raging thirst, the three men are simply too weak to continue. They lie close together, Scott and Bowers on either side of Wilson. Everything is tidy. Little passes between them. But there's comfort in being together when all chance of survival is lost. What little energy they have in reserve, they've used to write farewell letters. Bowers to his mother, Wilson to his wife. Scott has painstakingly written nine, despite there being no guarantee that their bodies will be found or the letters delivered.

Watching his handwriting deteriorate, his hand turning into an ever-clumsier instrument, Scott has pushed through the agony of exposing his bare skin to the sharp air of the tent to thank all those who helped him realise his ambitions. His failure to be first at the pole is of little consequence. What matters to Scott is the manner in which they have carried themselves – every single man. Together, they have taken on the greatest march ever made and come very near to great success; never giving up, and never giving up on each other. Of the friends, the men of influence he writes to, he asks that every effort be made to support the families these men leave behind. The sacrifice of those families is the greatest, and their burden all the more difficult to carry now that they are alone in the world.

Bowers is silent. Wilson has not stirred in many hours. Scott drags his body out of the sleeping bag to check on his friends. Both have finally surrendered to the cold. Death has come naturally, as they decided it would.

Scott removes his gloves and once more forces his pencil between his cold, stiffened fingers. He will write two more letters. It is the right thing to do, to tell Bowers's mother and Wilson's wife how their loved ones chose cheerfulness and bravery over panic and despair. For Scott, there are no tears to cry over his friends, only memories to cherish.

His diaries are complete. Factual. A full record. Of the battle they fought, and how death came in the end.

It seems a pity, but I do not think I can write more.

He signs his name and closes the book. He lies silent, contemplative. Again he picks up his pencil and scrawls one last message.

For God's sake look after our people.

Scott is not afraid. He allows his mind to dwell on humble pleasures – the sparkle of his wife's laughter, his son's breath warm on his cheek, the first bite of an apple plucked from the branch. Scott opens his sleeping bag and stretches his arm out over Wilson's body. What adventures they have had. What a story they could tell.

EPILOGUE

Was it a crevasse? Was it scurvy that took them? By late March, there is little doubt in the minds of those left at Cape Evans that, whatever the cause of death, Scott, Bowers, Wilson, Oates and Taff will never return.

The *Terra Nova* has already departed for New Zealand. Onboard are Meares, Ponting, Clissold, Simpson, Forde, Day, Anton, and Griffith Taylor. Lieutenant Evans, healthy enough to travel following his almost fatal bout of scurvy, has left Antarctica too. None of them is aware of the tragedy that has befallen their friends and their leader. None of them has heard Amundsen's news. Until they reach land, victory is still a possibility.

For those who have chosen to remain at Cape Evans, the winter is long. The landscape has lost its frozen appeal, the Southern Lights no longer inspire wonder. Their home is simply too cold, too dark and too lonely.

It is not until the end of October that a search party heads out across the Great Ice Barrier to find the lost southern party. Atkinson, Cherry-Garrard and Dimitri set off with two dog teams. Gran, Lashly, Crean, Hooper, Keohane, Nelson and Williamson lead the newly arrived mules. It feels just the same as last year. But instead of great expectations, the men face their journey with a sense of trepidation.

Two weeks in, they find the tent. Inside, three perfectly preserved bodies. Atkinson empties the men's pockets of their personal belongings. Scott's diary and a stack of letters are folded neatly under the Captain's head where they cannot be missed or overlooked. Carefully separating the pages, Atkinson reads Scott's account of their final weeks. He is shocked to learn of the hardships the men had to endure and of the immense suffering and bravery of Oates. Could they have done more, Atkinson wonders. It seems unlikely that anybody could have saved these wretched souls from the cruel winter blast that overtook the Barrier far earlier than all their weather records predicted. To perish so close to One Ton Depot, where ample fuel and food was waiting for them in the snow, was indeed a tragedy. If only they had marched one final day during their initial depot-laying mission, these men would still be alive.

Atkinson reads a passage from the Bible. The men lower the tent over the dead. Together they erect a cairn to commemorate the achievements of five friends and to mark the end of their astonishing polar journey.

For Gran, though, it is not enough. He straps on Scott's skis. There is a long journey ahead of him. His gift to the man he so admired is to complete the journey back to Cape Evans on ski as Scott would have wished, carrying the spirit of the great man with him.

APPENDICES

WINNER TAKES ALL – AMUNDSEN'S DASH TO THE POLE

The black flag that greeted Scott and his men when they reached 90 degrees south had been left by the Norwegian party on 14 December 1911. Tied to a discarded sledge runner, the flag was one of several markers Roald Amundsen had used to establish the precise location of the geographic South Pole. He had beaten Scott by thirty-four days.

The Norwegians enjoyed a relatively uneventful journey with none of the extreme weather and nightmarish snow conditions that had so tormented the British expedition. Leaving on 19 October from their winter base in the Bay of Whales, Amundsen and his men were some 100 kilometres closer to the pole than Cape Evans. After a week of efficient sledging, they had gained a further 240-kilometre advantage over Scott and his men, who would not even commence their journey until 1 November.

It took the Norwegians a total of twenty-six days to cross the Great Ice Barrier. With good weather and clear visibility, they were able to quickly establish a path up the as-yet unexplored Axel Heiberg Glacier and were already venturing forth across the polar plateau by 1 December 1911. Despite the difficulties posed by the thin air on the high-altitude plateau, Amundsen and his men encountered an even sledging surface and set a good pace for the last stage of their journey, reaching their goal a mere two weeks later.

Roald Amundsen, Oscar Wisting, Sverre Hassel, Helmer Hanssen and Olav Bjaaland would spend three days at Polheim, the name they gave their camp at the South Pole. It was critical that they demonstrate without a doubt that they had reached the correct spot. Without a discernable horizon and the sun barely deviating from its position overhead, the Norwegians could not entirely trust the accuracy of their instruments. Instead, Amundsen sent his men out 20 kilometres in three directions to take further observations. They had to be sure of their victory.

The dash south had been executed to plan, but it had not been an easy journey for the Norwegians. Freezing temperatures and savage wind had taken their toll on Amundsen's five-man party and the sled dogs that accompanied them. Frostbitten and with ravaged faces, the men were all daunted at the prospect of the return journey. Their survival was far from assured. For this reason alone, Amundsen sought Scott's help, requesting he oversee the delivery of his letter to the Norwegian king.

The weather was not the only unknown. The Norwegians were heavily reliant on dogs for their safe return home and the dogs were extremely hungry; ravenous to the point where they would eat anything vaguely edible – loose leather straps, boots or any pieces of clothing that lay within reach.

The dogs had undoubtedly been Amundsen's greatest advantage. Swift, light and resilient, they carried the men and their provisions much further each day than Scott and his manhaulers could manage. While less food would be needed for a quicker journey, Amundsen also knew that each dog represented 20 kilograms of fresh meat that would carry itself. When the time came, the dogs would be sacrificed to feed not only their canine companions but also the men who had driven them so far across an alien landscape where no living creature had ever passed before.

Amundsen had been worried about Scott. He knew the Englishman to be a capable and determined explorer who would stop at nothing to reach the southernmost point on Earth. Especially troubling for Amundsen was Scott's 'secret weapon', the motor sledges that just might carry him all the way to the pole and back. In the end he needn't have fretted.

The Norwegians and their eleven surviving dogs returned to the base at the Bay of Whales on 26 January 1912 and were picked up by their ship, the *Fram*, shortly after. Sailing into Hobart in early March, Amundsen was able to share news of his victory with the world. All his meticulous planning had paid off. The man who had conquered the North West Passage had once again scored a world first. However, this particular achievement would always be overshadowed by the death of Scott and his four men.

SCOTT'S DISCOVERY
EXPEDITION 1902–04

Even before his tragic death, Captain Scott was a household name in Britain, following his successful expedition to Antarctica aboard the *Discovery*, the first British vessel to be built for scientific exploration.

Organised by the Royal Geographical Society and financed by private and public donations, the expedition focused on an ambitious research program in the fields of magnetism, meteorology, geology, oceanography and biology over the course of a year.

Another key aim of the expedition was to build on the work of British polar explorer James Clark Ross, who discovered the Ross Sea. Venturing inland into those parts of Antarctica that could be easily reached was a particularly exciting prospect for Scott. Ascending in a hydrogen balloon to a height of 240 metres above the Great Ice Barrier, the young naval captain was awed and inspired by the vastness of the continent and its unknown nature that he hoped would reveal some of its mysteries in time.

With the *Discovery* safely moored in McMurdo Sound, the men established a series of shore huts where they could store equipment and emergency provisions and plan the many inland sledging excursions they hoped to make. Hut Point was the largest and would also serve as a shore base, should the men need to abandon the *Discovery*, which by late summer was already firmly frozen in the sea ice.

Having never visited the Antarctic, Scott was a complete novice; he lacked practical experience of polar travel and a true appreciation of the many risks to human survival in the polar regions. Adjustments to clothing, equipment and work practices were quickly adopted as both captain and crew came to respect their new hostile environment. The dangers of marching in white-out conditions became immediately apparent when a member of the crew, George Vince, stumbled over a precipice during a snowstorm. His body was never found.

The first winter aboard the *Discovery* passed well, with the crew easing into a work routine that was dictated by almost constant darkness. In the spring of 1902 an eager Scott set off with Wilson, Ernest Shackleton and a nineteen-strong dog team to see how far they could venture towards the South Pole.

It was an audacious attempt. They knew nothing of their route or what perils awaited in the interior. They achieved a new 'furthest south' record before their luck took a turn for the worse. Suffering from snow blindness, weakened by constant hunger and disappointed in their dogs, Scott, Wilson and Shackleton were nevertheless reluctant to turn back. Feeble pullers already, the dogs were succumbing to exhaustion. The ones that dropped by the wayside were readily eaten by their companions.

The dogs were not the only ones failing. By late December, it was clear to Wilson that Ernest Shackleton was displaying the early signs of scurvy. They were at the limit of their endurance. On 30 December the men reached 82 degrees south – a massive achievement and a new record. A speedy return was critical for all of them, but particularly Shackleton, who was now breathing with difficulty and coughing up blood.

The few remaining dogs were of no help and now trailed the men as they hauled their own sledge. Shackleton's health had deteriorated and he could no longer walk. To lighten their load, the men were forced to dump the remaining dog food and kill their two surviving dogs. Towing their friend to safety nearly finished Wilson and Scott off, but it also cemented a friendship that would see them through to the end many years later.

A long recuperation for Wilson and Shackleton followed aboard the *Discovery*, which was still firmly wedged in the sea ice despite the warm summer months. Luckily a relief ship, *Morning*, had arrived to replenish supplies and accompany the *Discovery* back to civilisation.

When blasting with explosives failed to dislodge the *Discovery*, Scott resigned himself to a second winter on the ice. A number of men were sent home aboard the *Morning*, including Shackleton, who despite poor health was desperate to stay on in Antarctica and finish the work he had started. He would lead his own expedition in 1908.

Having made a full recovery, Wilson ventured forth at the tail end of their second winter in Antarctica to the penguin colony at Cape Crozier. Where he hoped to gather eggs, Wilson found a hundred adults and many chicks. Clearly too late, Dr Wilson would have to make a return to the penguin rookery in mid-winter if he was to collect his precious specimens. The dangerous journey he would eventually make with Cherry and Bowers would prove almost as much of a disappointment.

Meanwhile, Scott set out to explore further regions with a group of men that included Taff Evans and William Lashly. When conditions deteriorated, forcing the others to turn back, only Scott, Taff and Lashly continued their quest into the unknown. During the homeward journey, Scott, Taff and the sledge plummeted into a crevasse. In an astonishing feat of strength, Lashly held on to all three until Scott and Taff could clamber to safety. The admiration Scott felt for his two strapping travelling companions would ultimately assure the men places on his next Antarctic expedition aboard the *Terra Nova*.

When summer returned, the *Discovery* remained resolutely stuck in McMurdo Sound. Facing the prospect of a third winter on the ice, every man engaged in sawing a path through the 32 kilometres of ice that lay between *Discovery* and the open sea. Again the *Morning* arrived – this time accompanied by a second relief ship, the *Terra Nova*.

After frantic attempts and further blasting with explosives, Scott drew up plans to abandon the vessel that had been their home for almost two years. Only then did the seemingly impossible happen. Leads opened up and with one final push the *Discovery* was free to return to Great Britain with its wealth of Antarctic knowledge and bounty of scientific discoveries. Scott would return a hero and his life would never be the same.

SHACKLETON'S ATTEMPT ON THE POLE 1908-09

It was with a heavy heart that Ernest Shackleton left Antarctica in 1903 aboard the relief ship *Morning*. Scott had ordered his return due to his poor state of health.

Shackleton cried openly on leaving. A lover of adventure, he had fallen under the spell of the great white continent. There was so much that remained unexplored, that lay unknown and yet within reach of a tenacious individual like himself. Besides, the greatest prize – the South Pole – was yet to be claimed.

Back in London, Shackleton worked tirelessly to raise funds and convince influential people to support an expedition of his own. Years passed. Success seemed to be lurking just beyond his reach. But Shackleton's determination paid off. In February 1907 he announced his return to Antarctica. Funds were seriously short but, forever optimistic, Shackleton knew he could make it work. Four hundred men applied to join him aboard the *Nimrod*, a forty-year-old sealing vessel with rotting masts. Only fifteen would be chosen to winter on the ice.

After being towed a staggering 2400 kilometres from New Zealand by another ship in an effort to conserve fuel, the *Nimrod* finally reached Antarctica towards the end of January 1908. Finding a safe landing spot proved difficult. The Barrier edge had crumbled away since *Discovery* days and it was obviously too unstable to establish any kind of base on as Shackleton had hoped. Another potential landing spot, Hut Point, was barred by 32 kilometres of solid sea ice. With no other options, the men resolved to build a winter camp at Cape Royds on Ross Island.

Hopes were high when Shackleton, three of his men and their ponies set out for the pole in November 1908. They carried food for ninety-one days, but from early on it became apparent that the powdered beef, wheat meal biscuits, sugar, cheese and chocolate would not sustain their massive energy needs. They shot a horse, burying what meat they couldn't eat. They would dig it up on their return journey like hungry dogs.

The mental strain of their journey weighed enormously on each of them. Day after day they pushed themselves through the deep snowy silence, with a never-setting sun illuminating an unchanging and featureless landscape before them. Two more ponies were shot. The men talked endlessly of their favourite foods, of the restaurants they would visit and the elaborate meals they would order. Crevasses – some deep, some wide, many of them concealed beneath the fragile surface crust, were a constant threat. One lay hidden, just outside the tent flap. Another almost swallowed the cooking gear and rations and one of Shackleton's men. On the Beardmore Glacier their last pony disappeared into a crevasse so deep that no sign of the animal remained, and no telltale sounds of its sad fate escaped the icy chasm.

Knowing that it was increasingly unlikely they would ever reach the pole, the men carried on in their quest, hopeful of making a new 'furthest south' record. Already by December they had passed the point where Shackleton, Scott and Wilson had decided to turn back. Every day on the polar plateau represented a frightful ordeal with barely enough oxygen, razor-sharp headwinds cutting through clothing and the blood freezing in their hands and feet.

'The end is in sight,' Shackleton finally admitted in his journal at the beginning of January 1909. 'We can only go for three more days at the most, for we are weakening rapidly.' Hunger was the enemy. Lacking food and fuel, the men could venture no further.

On 9 January the men set off without their sledge to forge on as far as they could from their camp towards the South Pole. Together they achieved a new record of 88 degrees south, an incredible feat that would transform them into national heroes, despite falling 180 kilometres short of their goal.

Even though he failed to reach the actual pole, Shackleton had built on the knowledge gained during his earlier attempt with Scott and Wilson, and had learnt many hard lessons of his own. Consequently, Shackleton's account of the *Nimrod* expedition was studied in great depth by Captain Scott when planning his *Terra Nova* expedition. What Shackleton had almost accomplished, Scott had every intention of finishing.

It was clear that food had been their downfall. If Shackleton and his men failed because they could not physically take enough food to support their final push, then it seemed a reasonable assumption that a larger support team would be needed to haul adequate provisions.

Shackleton's choice of ponies also played an enormous part in Scott's planning. While Scott had experienced only trouble and frustration with the dog teams during the *Discovery* attempt, Shackleton had modest success with the pulling power of his ponies, which then became a valuable source of food. Ponies were not as fast as dogs, but speed was not the issue for Scott. The epic journey he was planning had not yet become a race.

Undeterred by Scott's death or Amundsen's victory, Shackleton returned to Antarctica in 1914 to complete what would surely have been one of the greatest polar journeys ever attempted – a 2900-kilometre journey across the continent from the Weddell Sea at the foot of the Atlantic Ocean to the Ross Sea on the other side of the globe.

As it turned out, not one man stepped ashore, but the remarkable story of the *Endurance* and her crew has become one of the greatest tales of survival of modern times.

GLOSSARY

Finnesko – Reindeer-hide boots. The furry outside provides grip on snow and ice.

Great Ice Barrier – Now known as the Ross Ice Shelf.

Hoosh – A runny stew made from a random collection of ingredients (usually pemmican) mixed up with water and heated through.

Leads – A fracture in an expanse of sea ice that allows ships to pass with greater ease.

Pemmican – Sledging rations made from dried meat pounded to a paste, mixed with fat and compressed into high-energy, high-protein blocks. May be eaten as is or mixed with water to form a thin soup.

Ratings – An enlisted member of the navy, subordinate to officers.

Sastrugi – 'Waves' of hardened snow of varying sizes and shapes that form on polar plains.

Taff – The nickname of Petty Officer Edgar Evans; used in this book to avoid confusion with Scott's second-in-command, Lieutenant Edward 'Teddy' Evans.

Theodolite – An instrument for measuring horizontal and vertical angles, used most often by Lieutenant Bowers to establish elevation and measure distance.

BIBLIOGRAPHY

Amundsen, Roald, *The South Pole: an account of the Norwegian Antarctic expedition in the Fram 1910–1912*, John Murray, London, 1912

Cherry-Garrard, Apsley, *The Worst Journey in the World*, Vintage, London, 2010

Fiennes, Ranulph, *Captain Scott*, Hodder & Stoughton, London, 2003

MacPhee, Ross D.E., *Race to the End – Scott, Amundsen and the South Pole*, Natural History Museum, London, 2011

Mountfield, David, *A History of Polar Exploration*, The Hamlyn Publishing Group, London, 1974

Ponting, Herbert G., *The Great White South: or with Scott in the Antarctic*, Gerald Duckworth, London, 1921

Scott, Robert F., *The Last Expedition*, Vintage Publishing, London, 2013

Turney, Chris, *1912 – The Year the World Discovered Antarctica*, Text Publishing, Melbourne, 2012

Wilson, David M., *The Lost Photographs of Captain Scott*, Hachette, London, 2011

ACKNOWLEDGEMENTS

I would like to express my sincere thanks to the team at Allen & Unwin Melbourne, in particular Erica Wagner for sharing her early enthusiasm for the project and Kate Whitfield, my talented editor, for her months of hard work, her many thoughtful suggestions for the text and the uncompromising approach she has taken to the look and feel of *Into the White*. I also extend heartfelt thanks to Sarah Lippett for her wonderful illustrations and her willingness to be involved with the book from the very early stages.

Many people have been unwittingly part of the writing process. I would like to thank Hilary Stichbury for the years of friendship and encouragement, and Kimberly Sumner for the many uplifting conversations that served to kick-start my working day. My gratitude also extends to my earliest reader Issie Cunningham for her close reading and feedback, as well as to Maria Konings and Suzy Fraser for kindly offering to read the finished manuscript.

My parents, Helen and Bill Cunningham, have provided endless encouragement and shown constant interest in the research and writing of this story. I am deeply grateful to them for always engaging and never tiring of the subject matter.

Finally to Pawel, Kazik and Ziggy I say thank you for the countless ways you bring joy to my life. Your unwavering love and support makes anything possible.

ABOUT THE AUTHOR

Joanna Grochowicz has a background in foreign languages and literature and has enjoyed a varied career working with words in both corporate and not-for-profit sectors. *Into the White* is her first book.